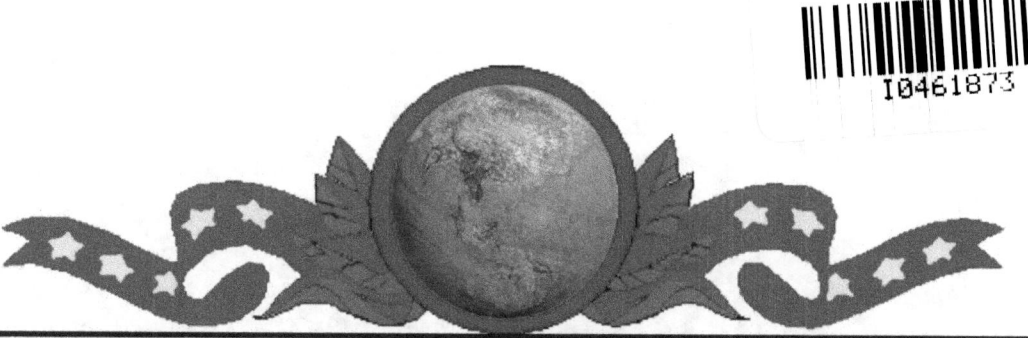

Real World
Colouring Book
For Advanced Users & Adults

Copyright 2019 By John Boom

50 Images

Created From Real Life Photos
For You To Colour As You Please.

ISBN 978-0-359-82341-3

9 780359 823413

90000

I0461873

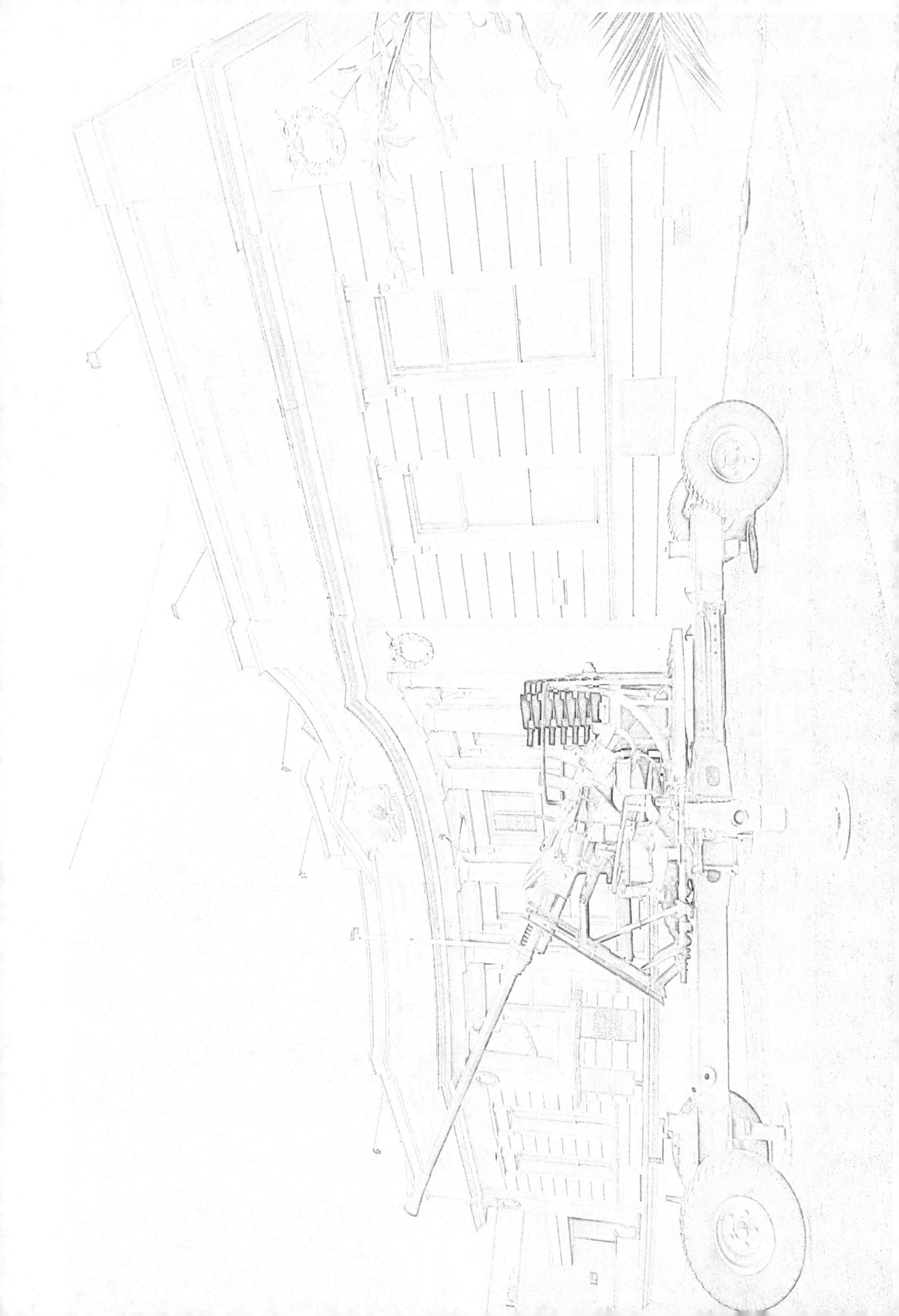

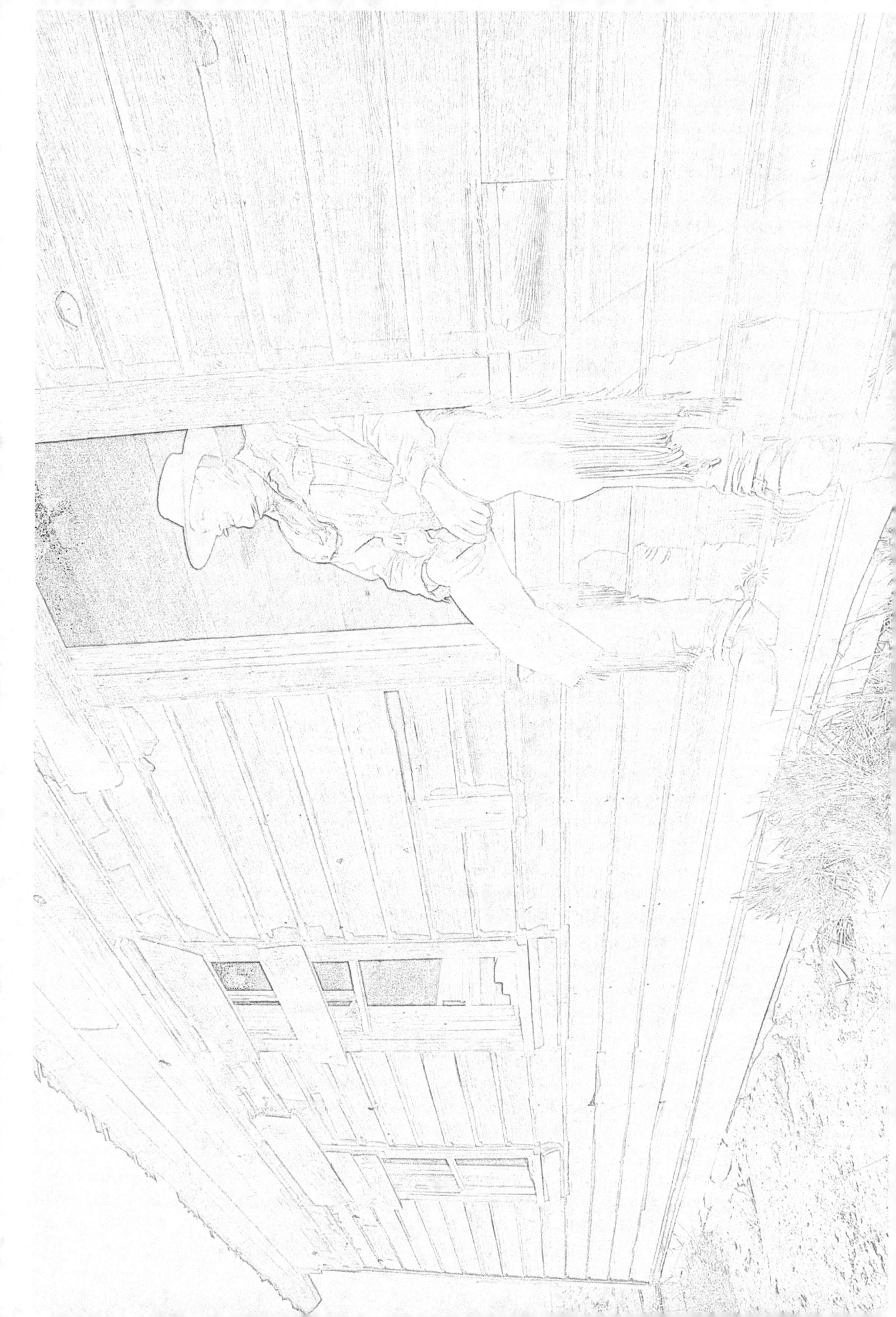

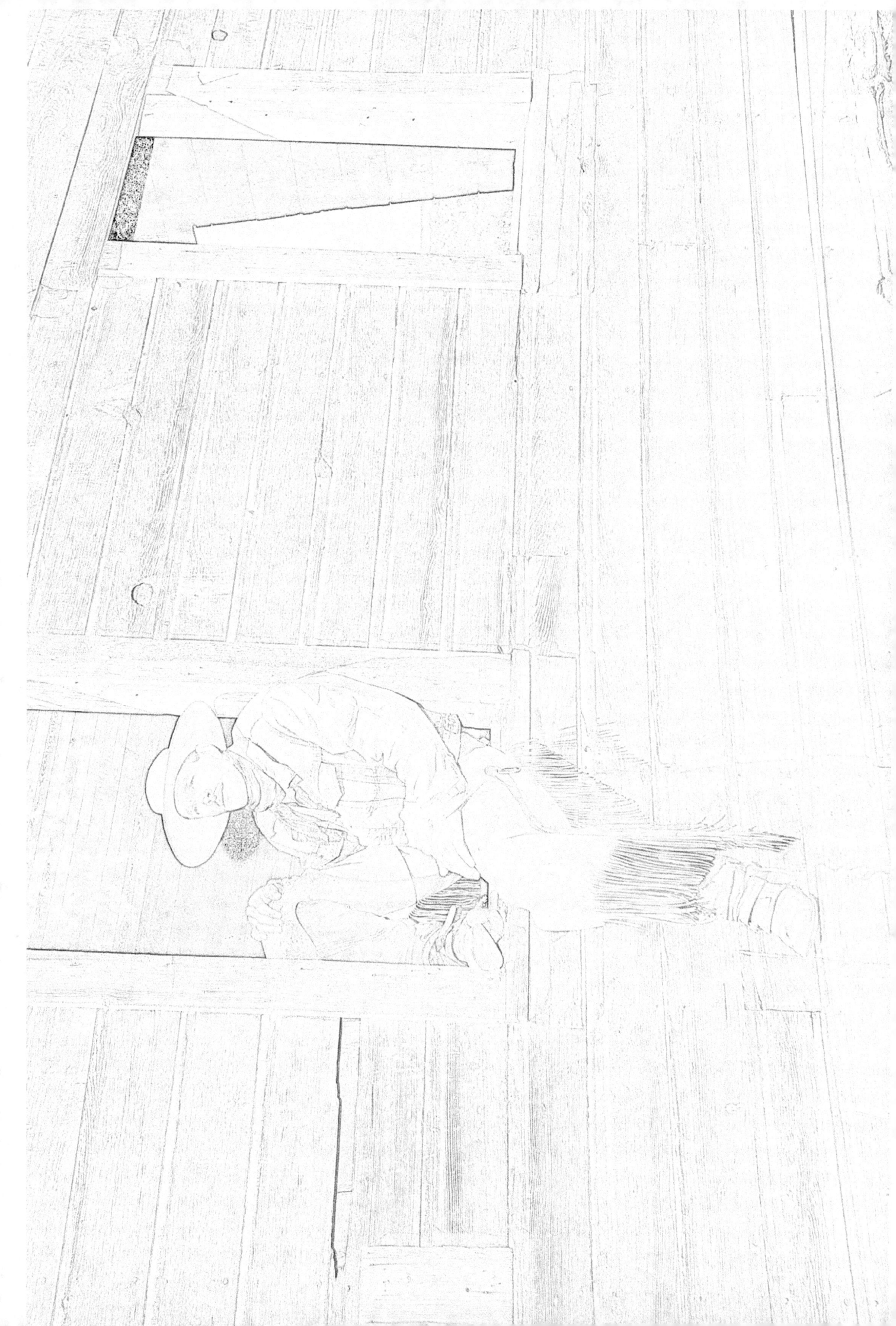

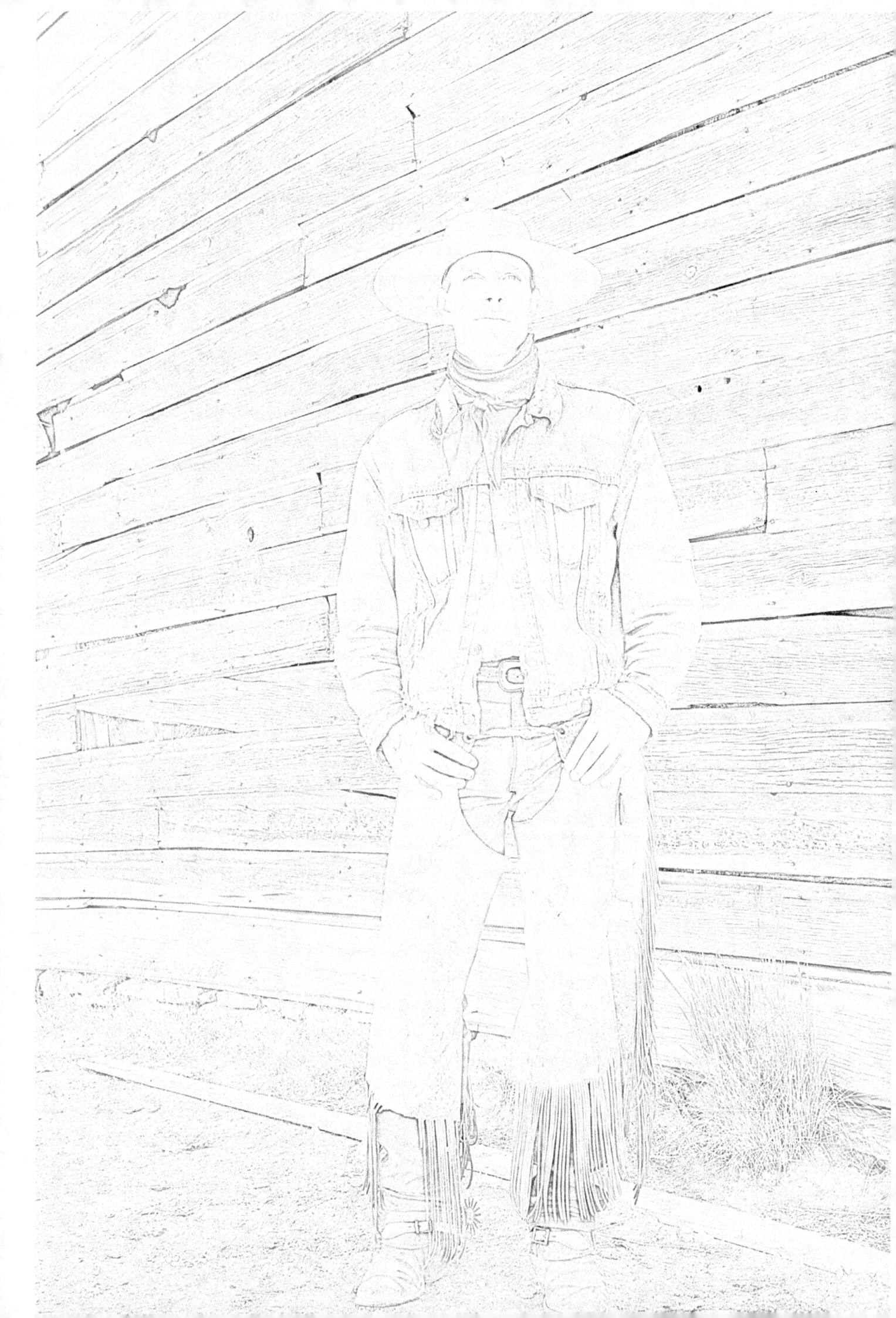

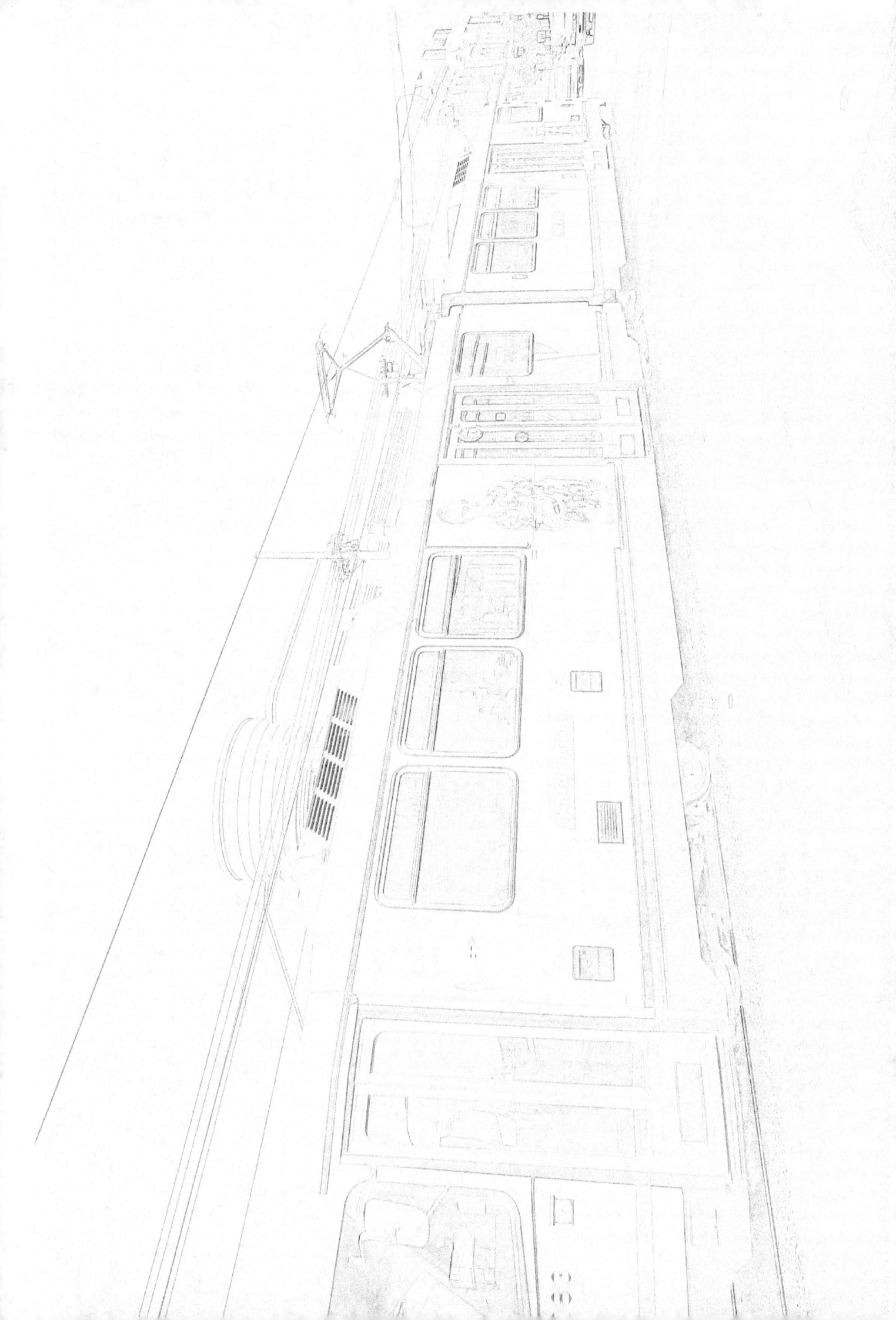

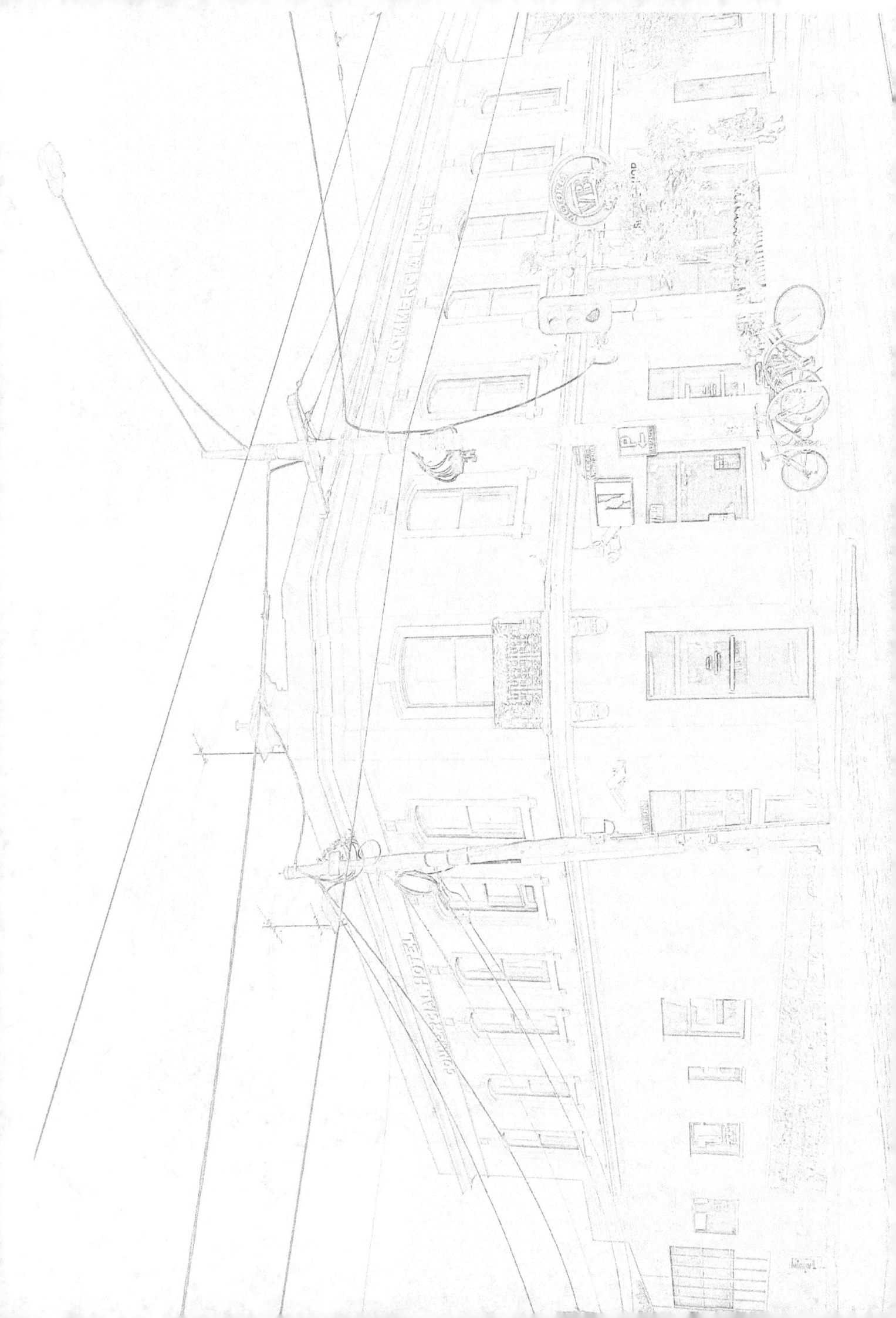

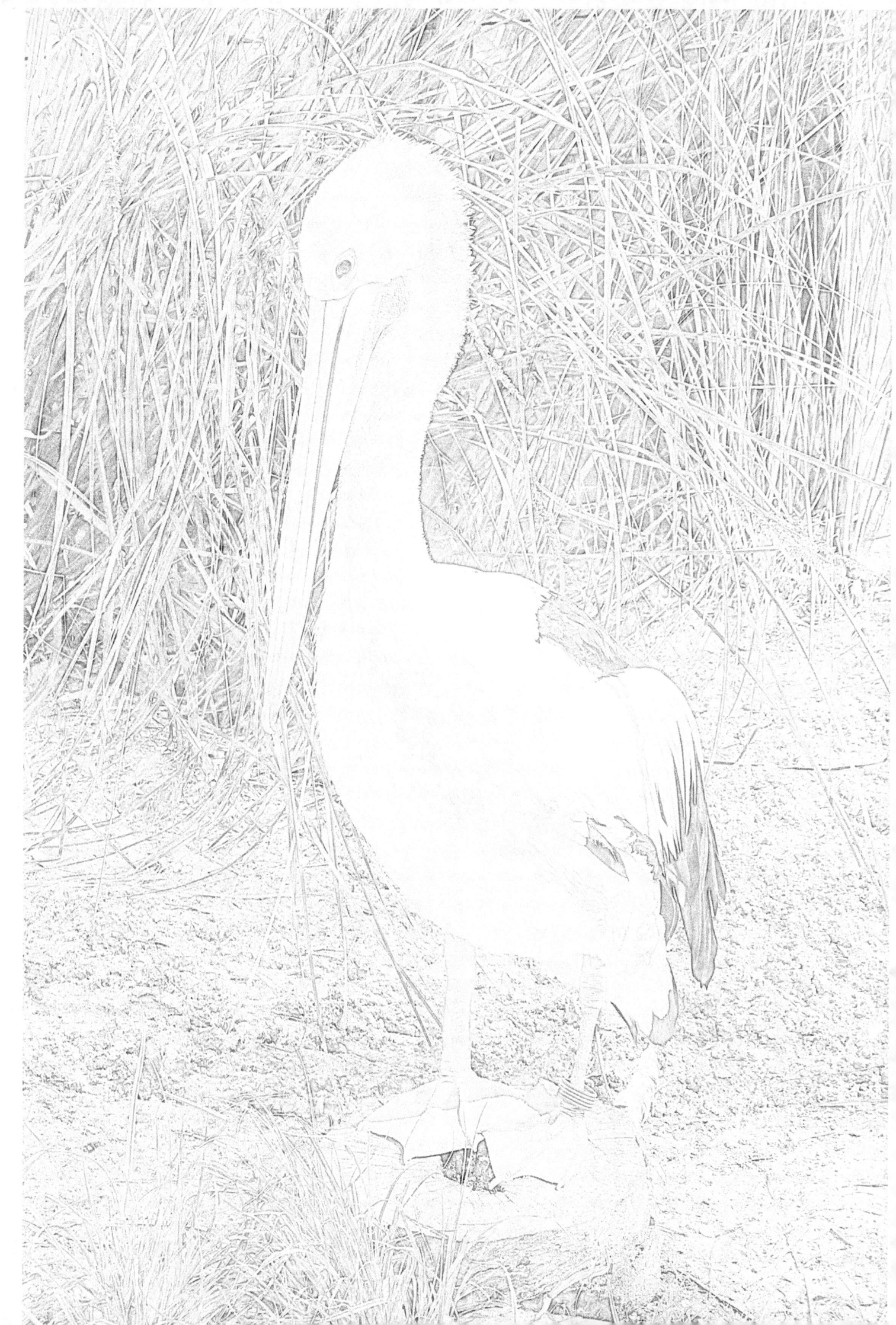

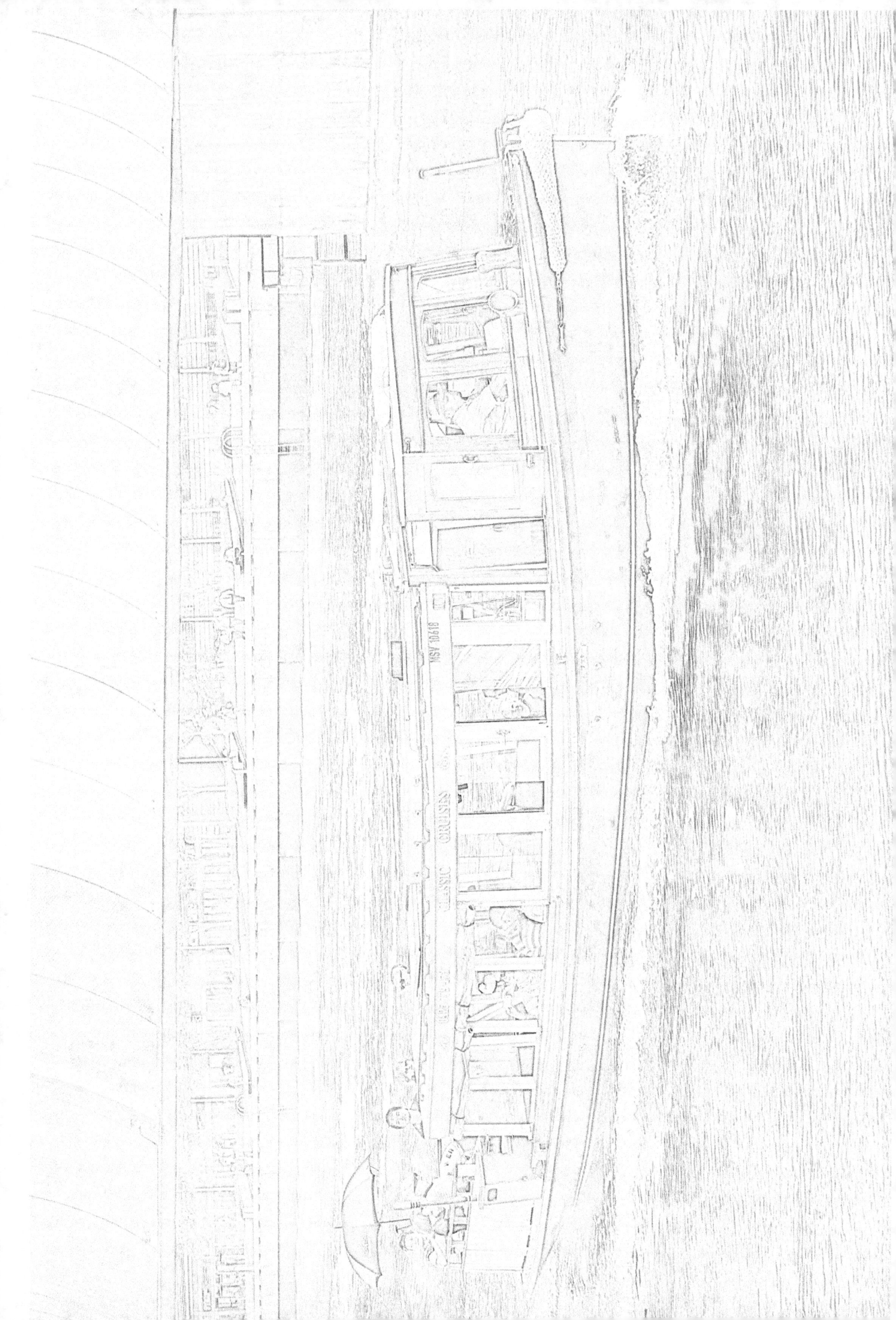

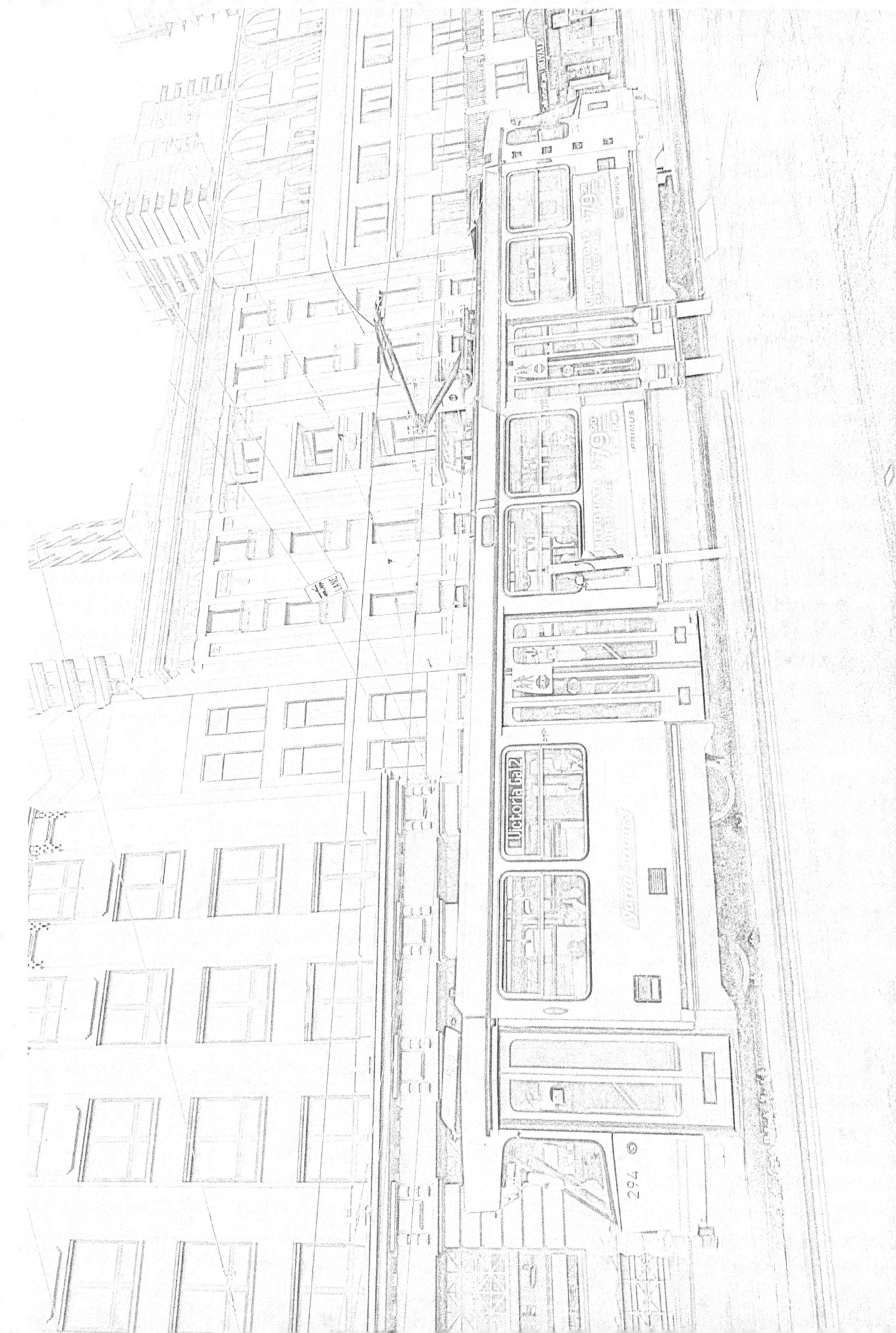

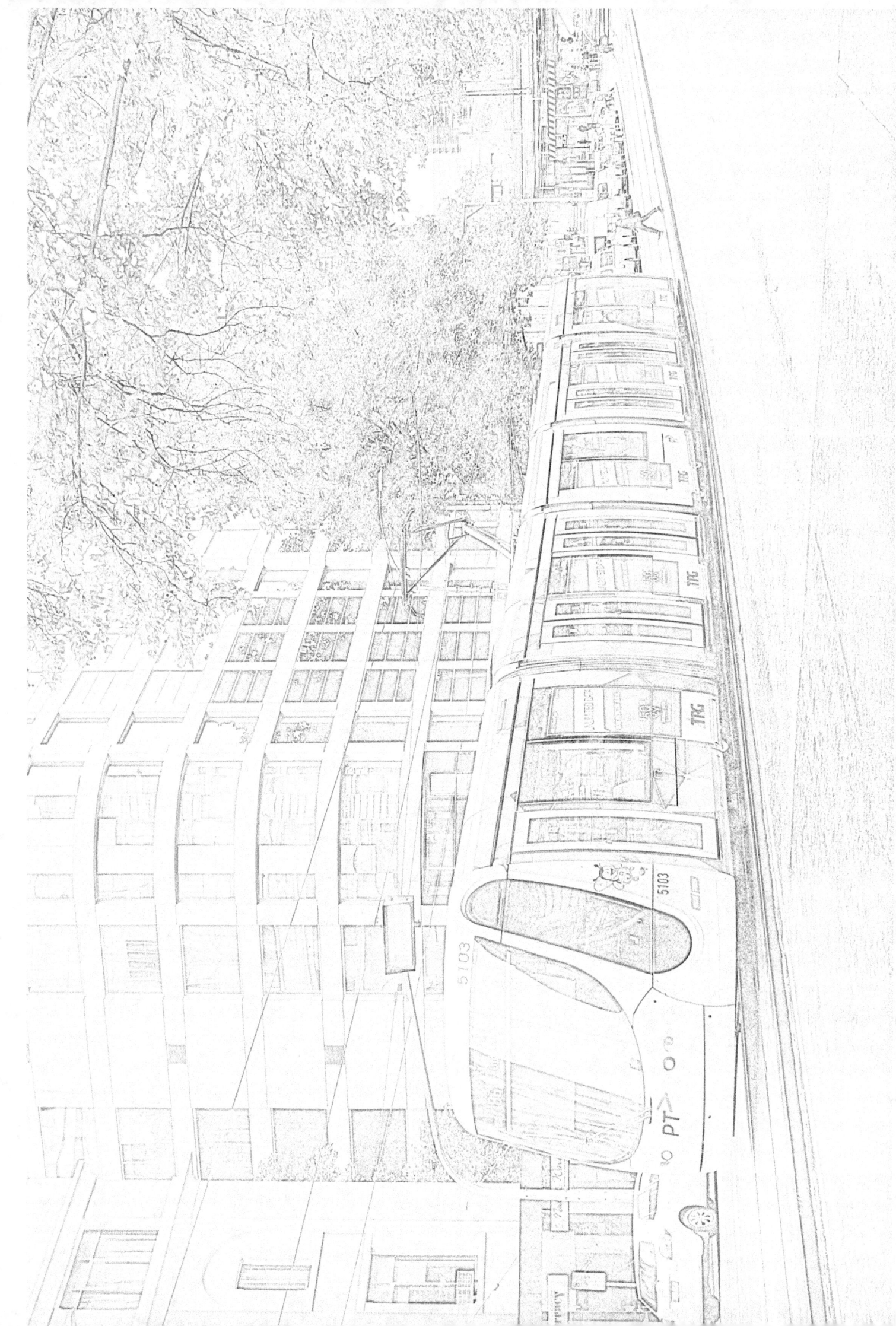

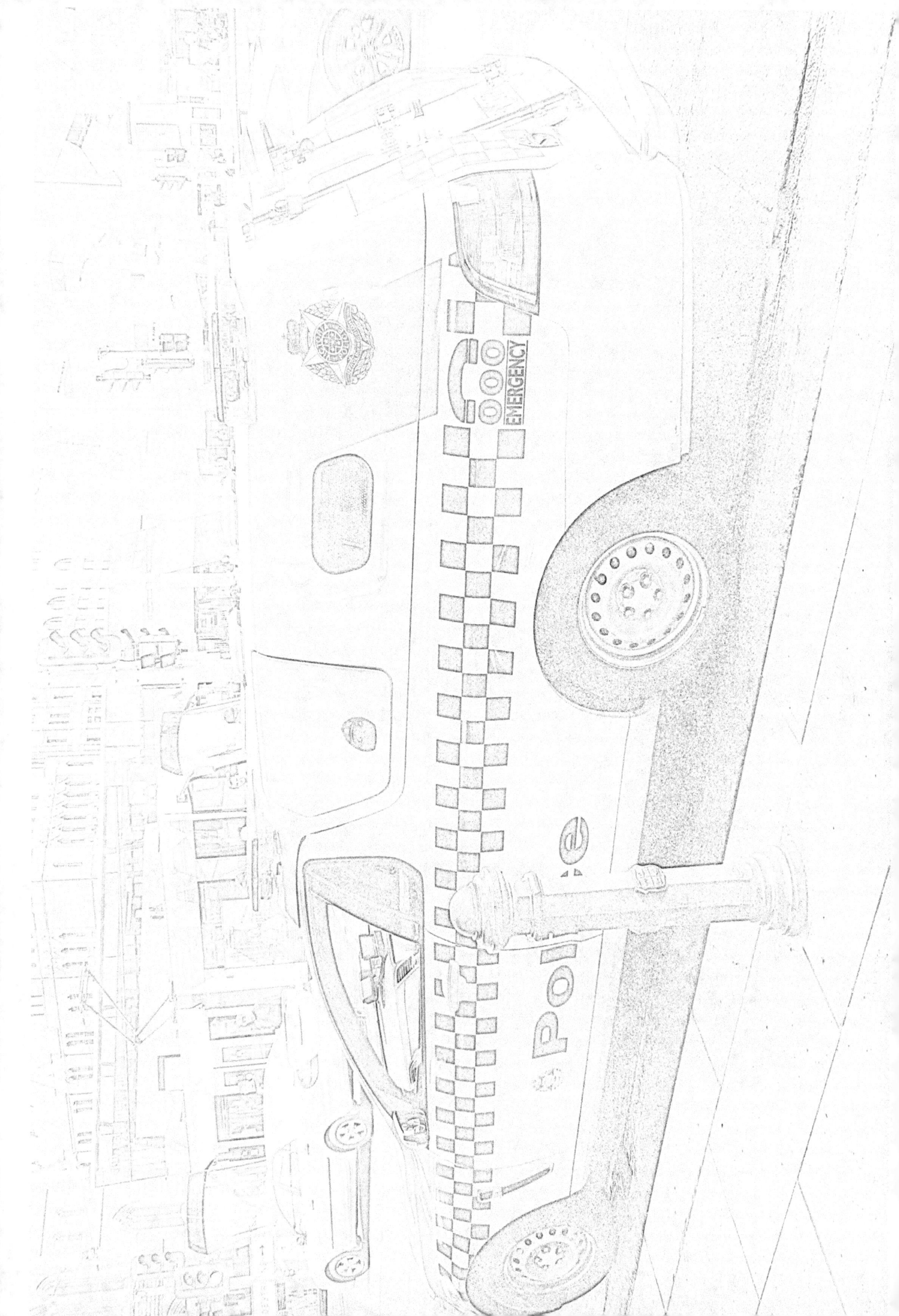

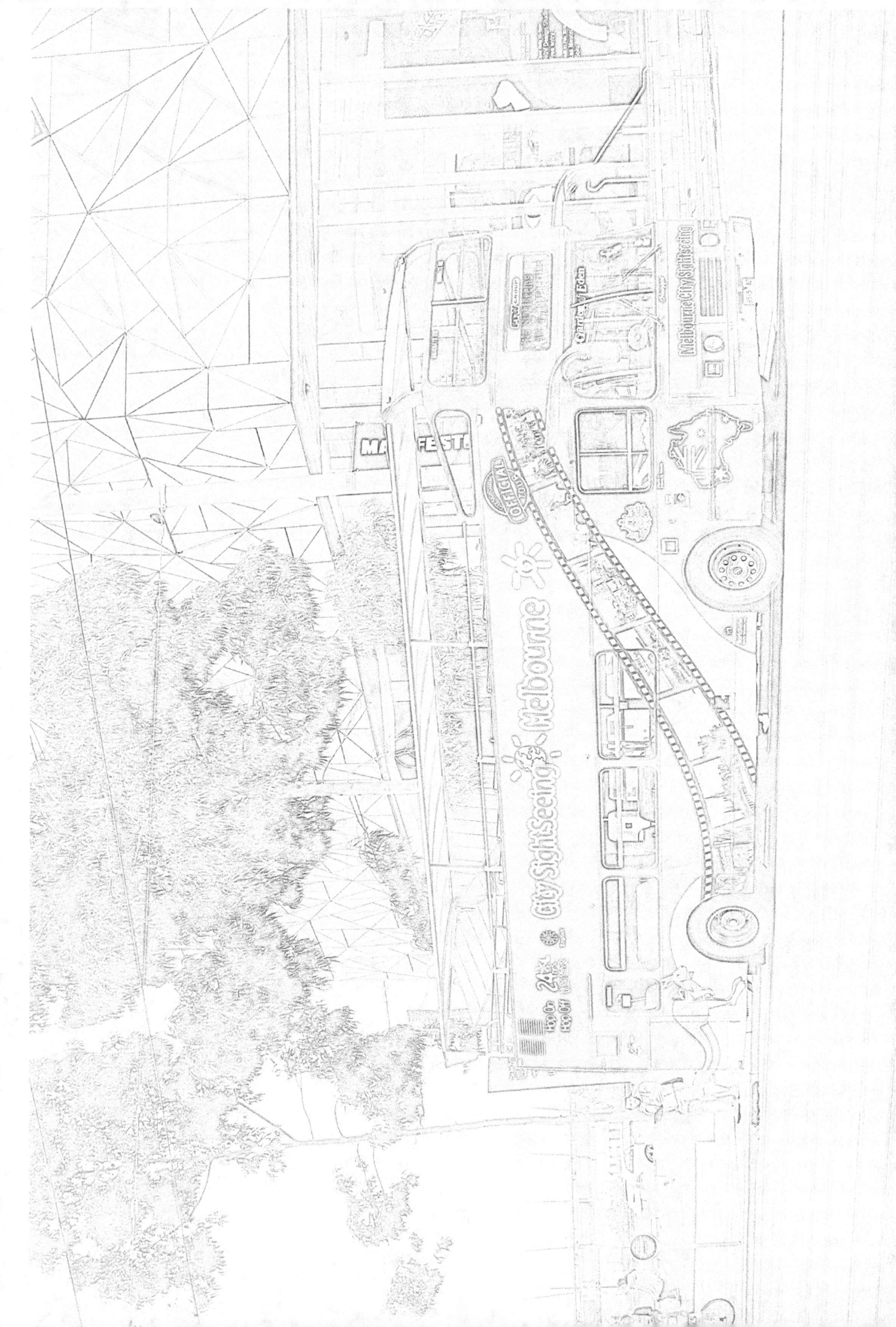

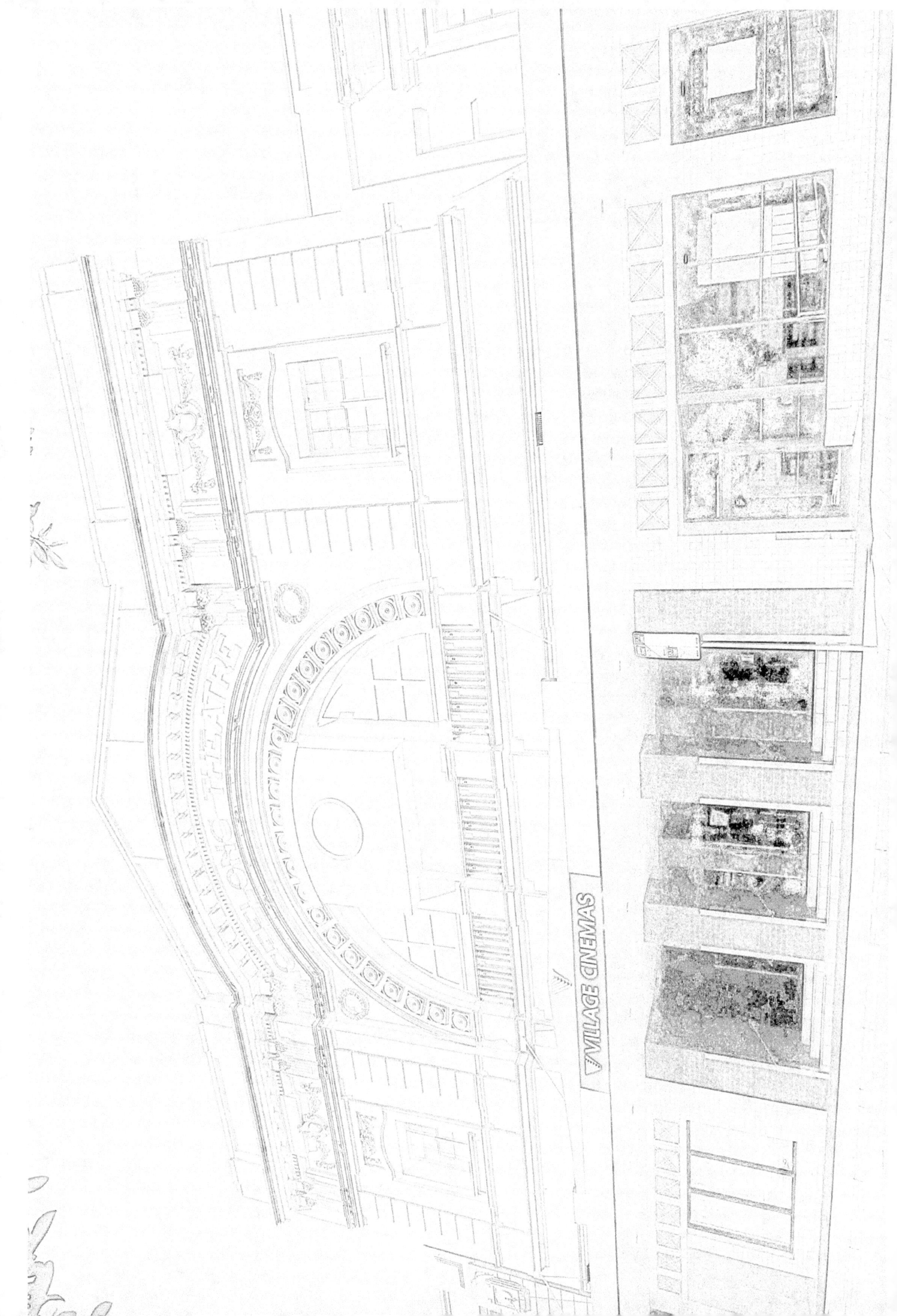

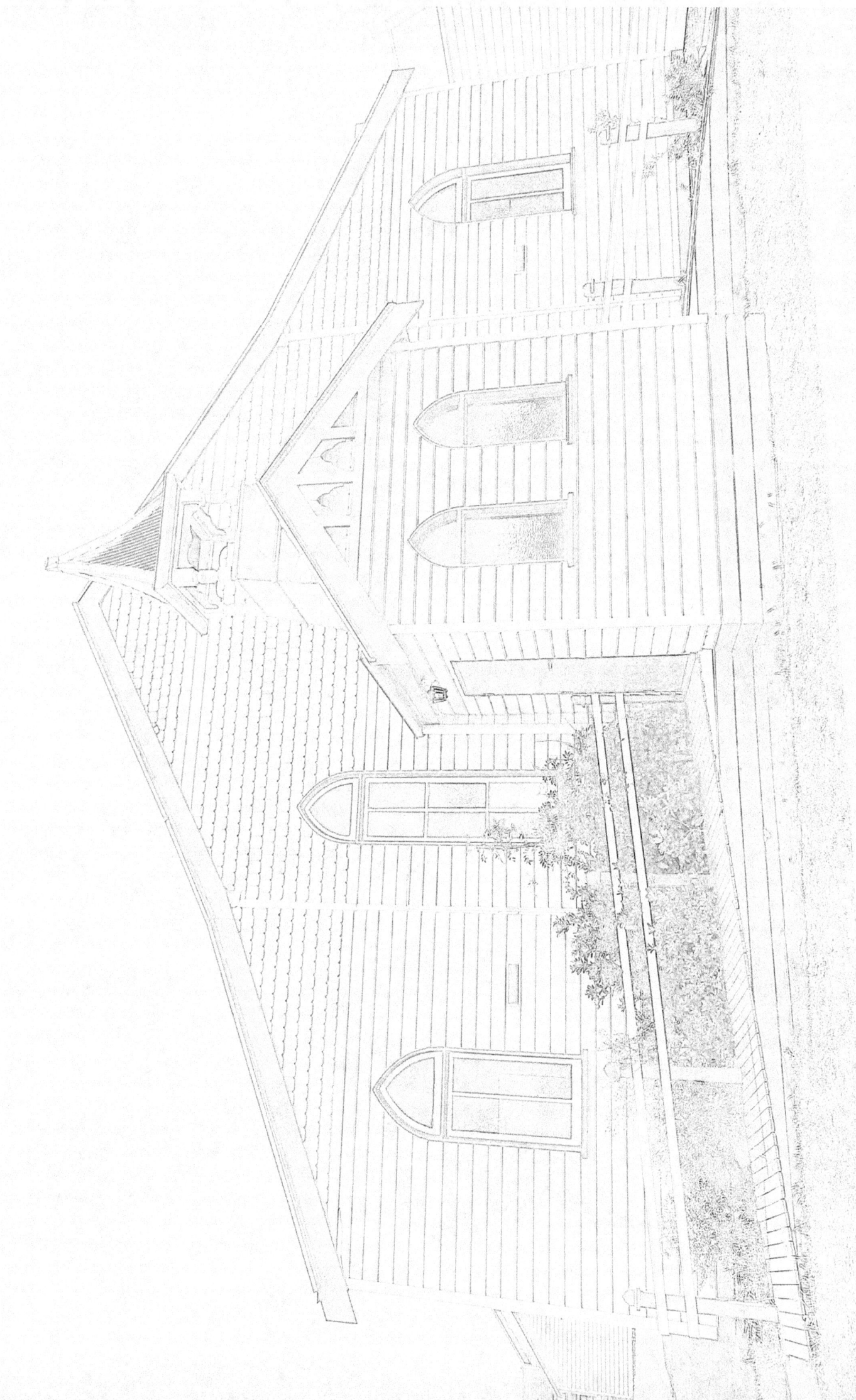

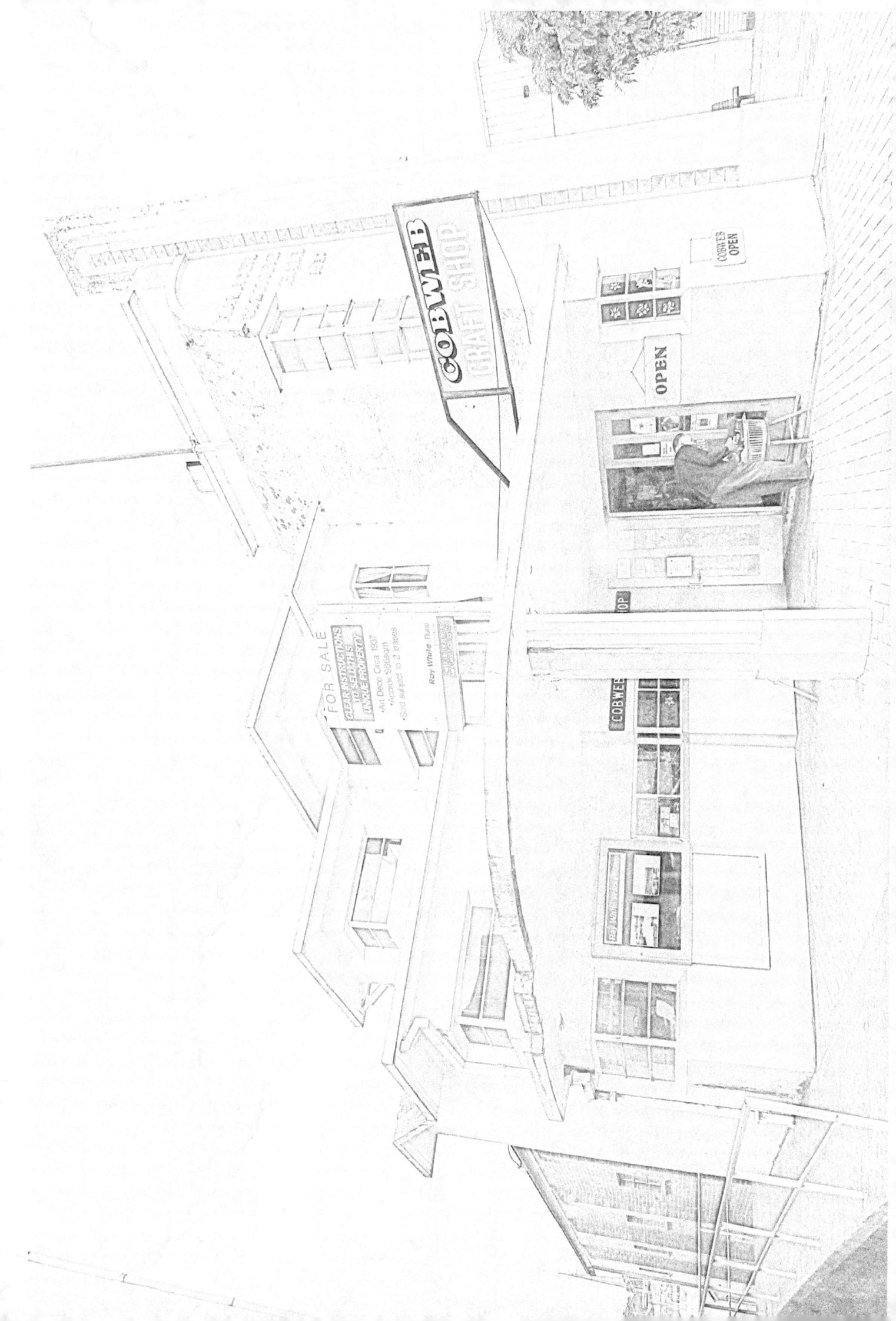

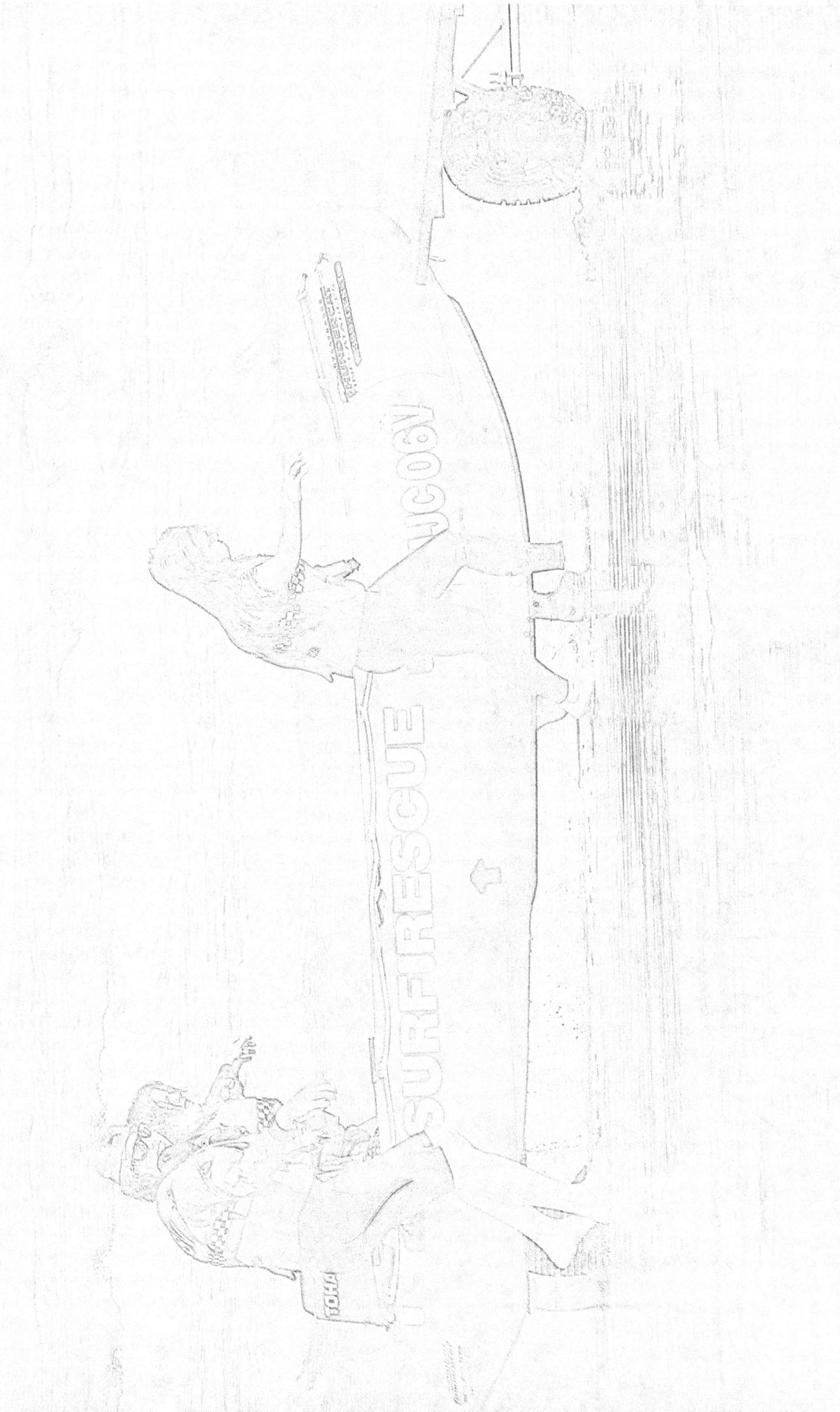

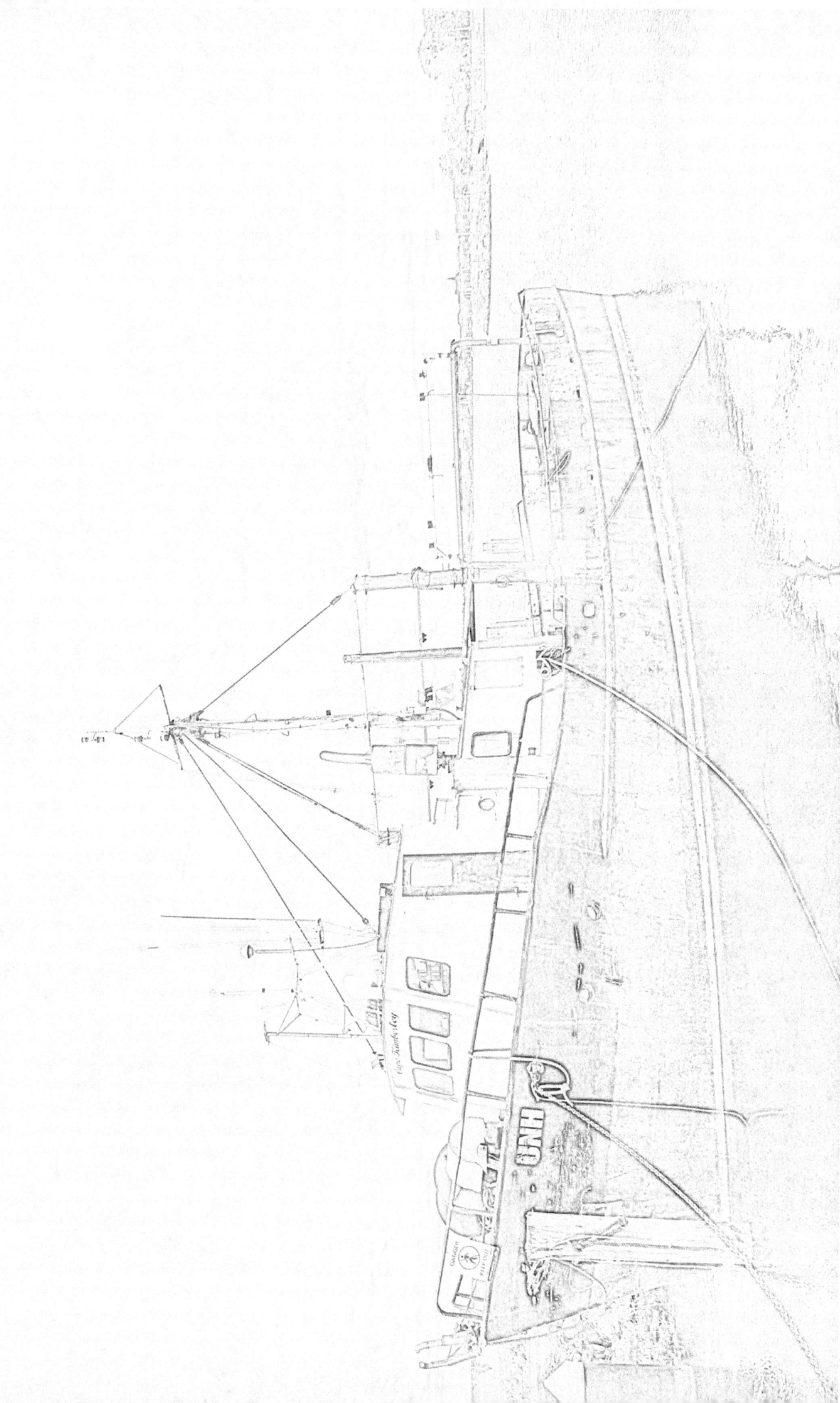

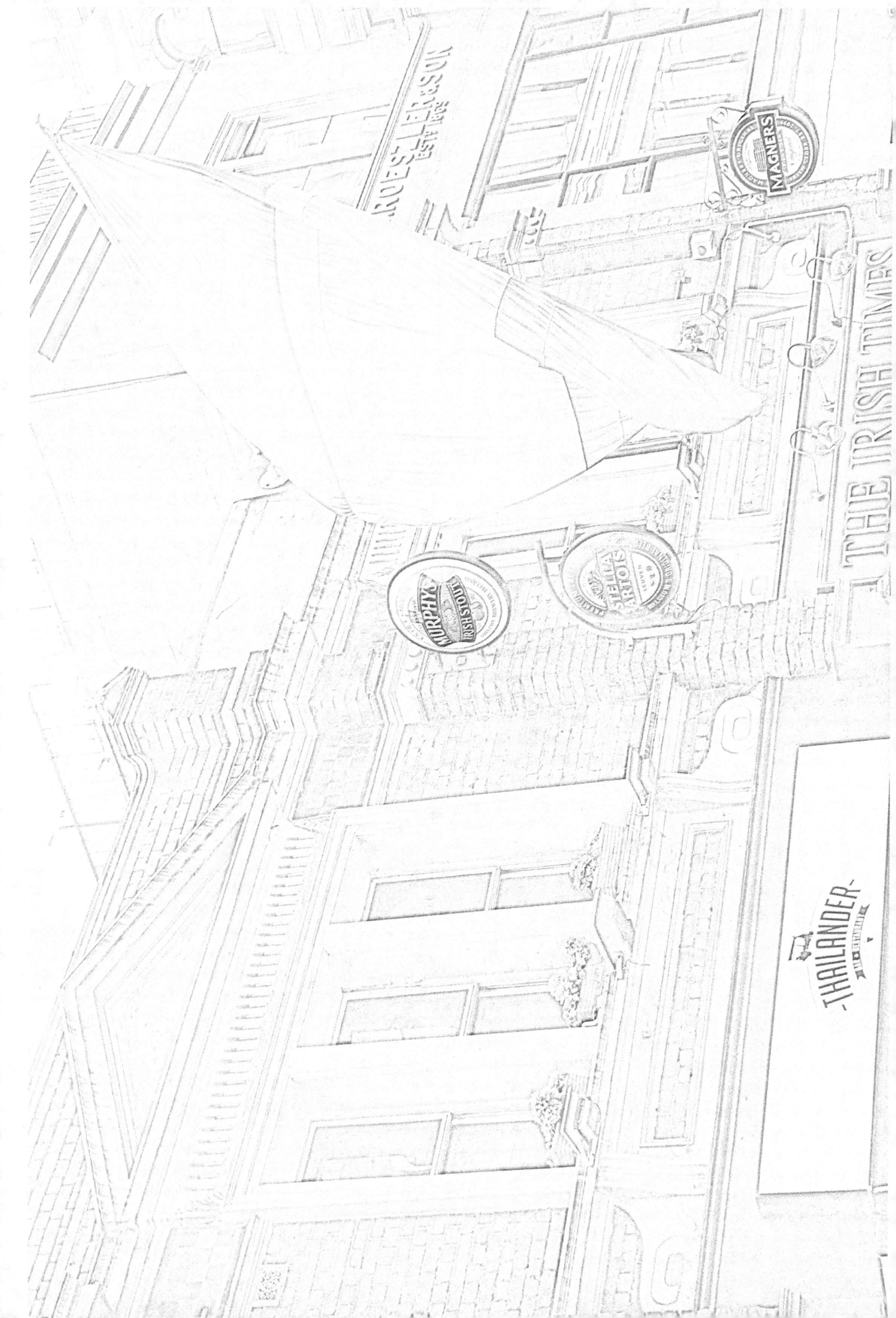

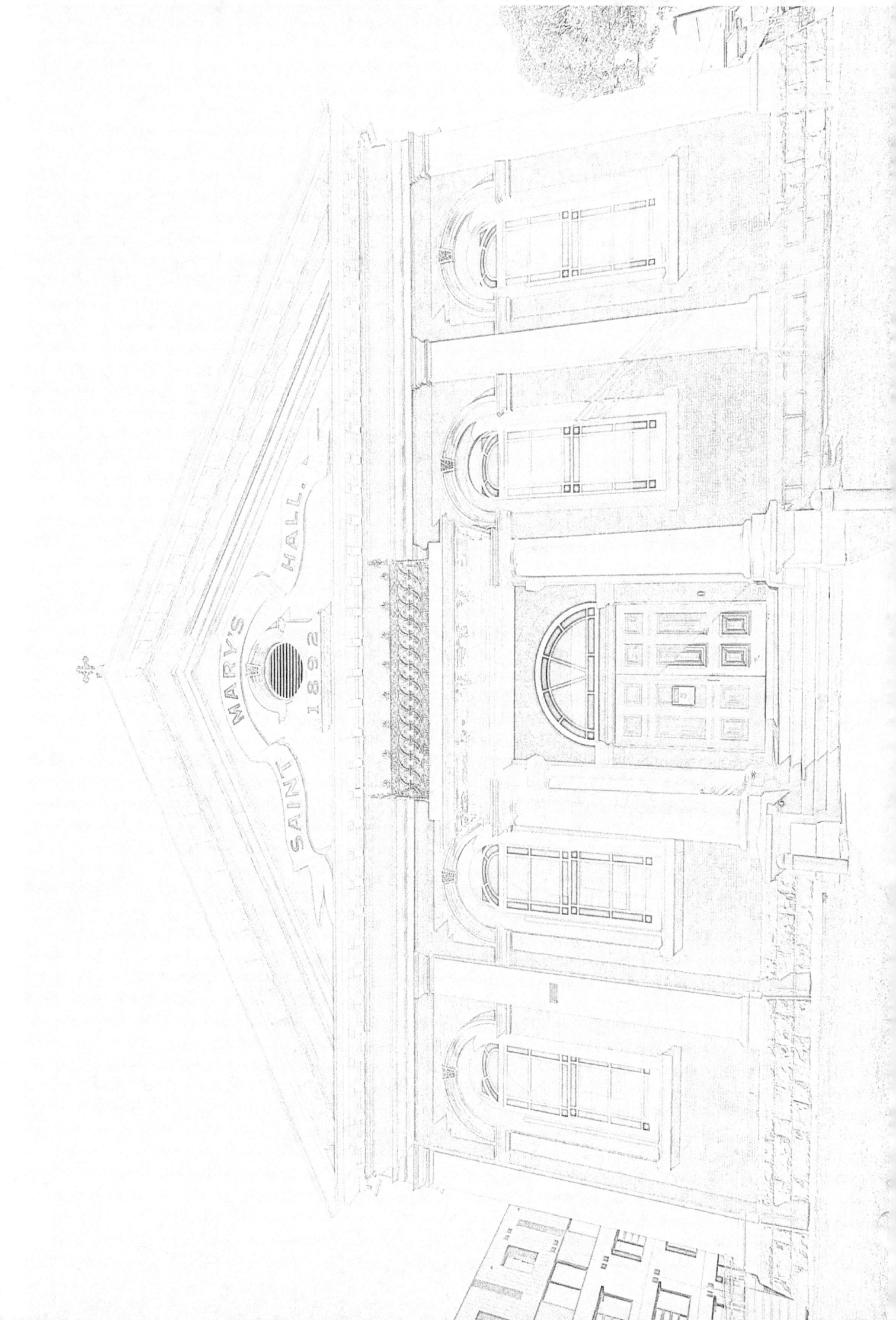

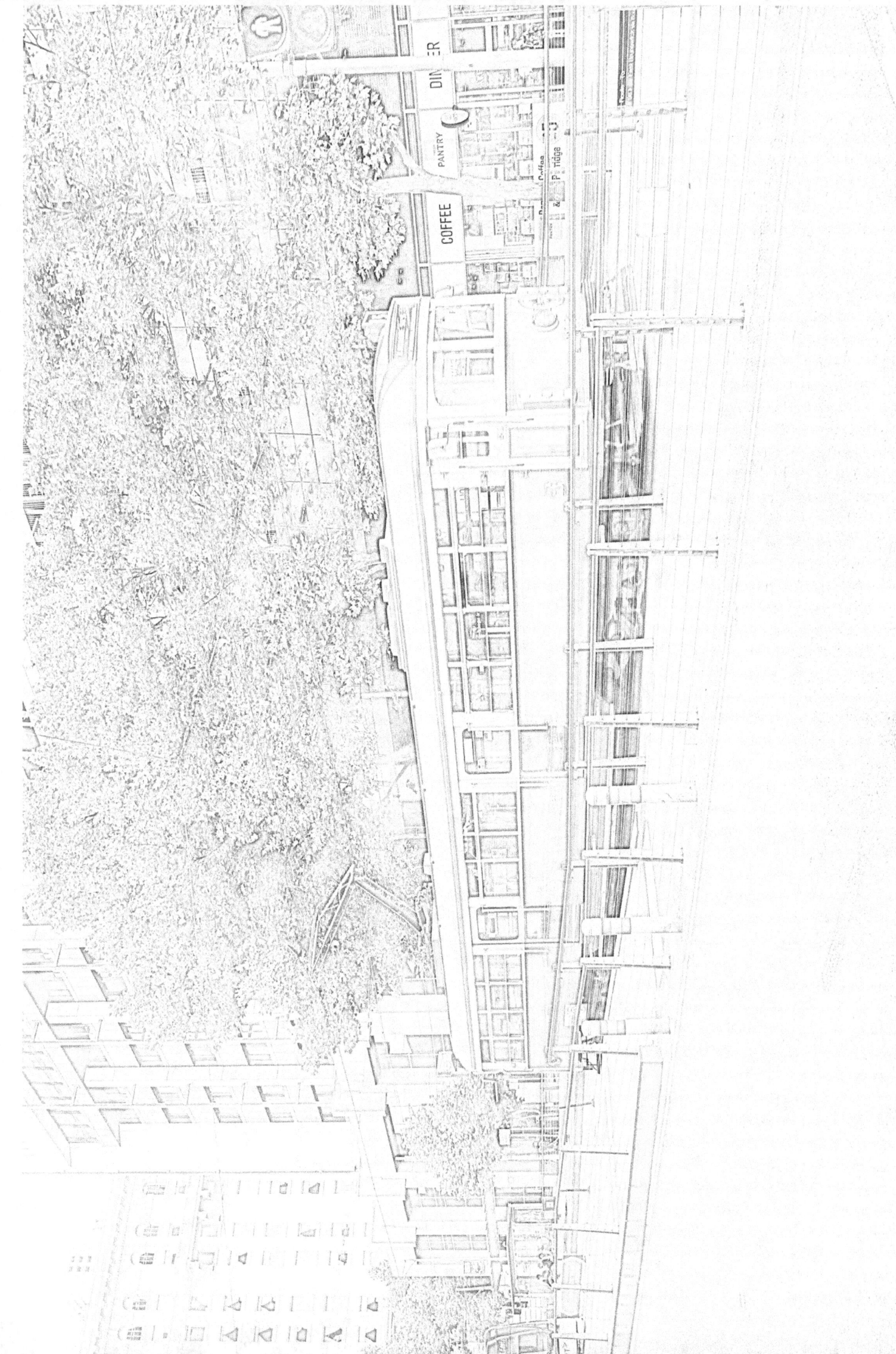

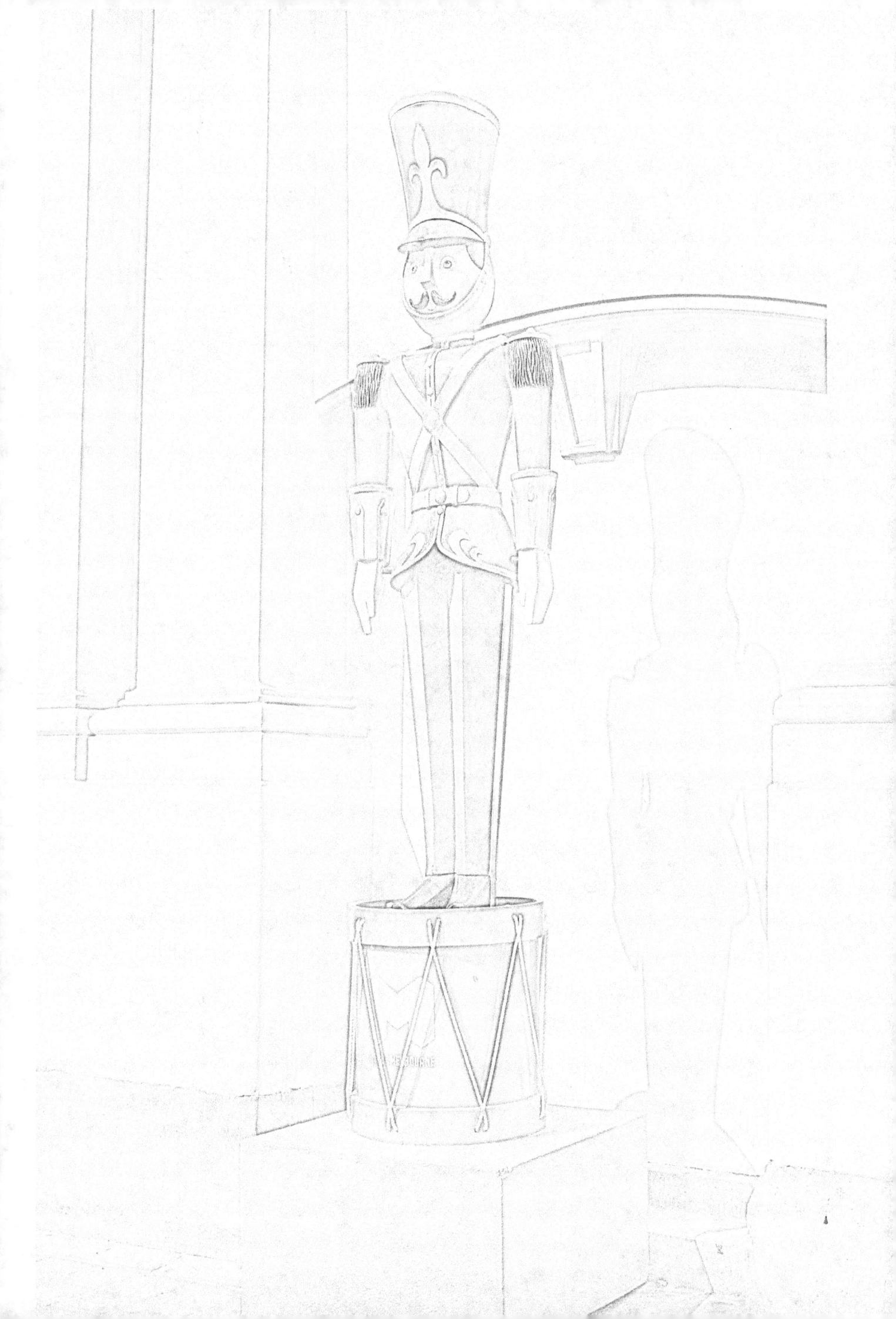

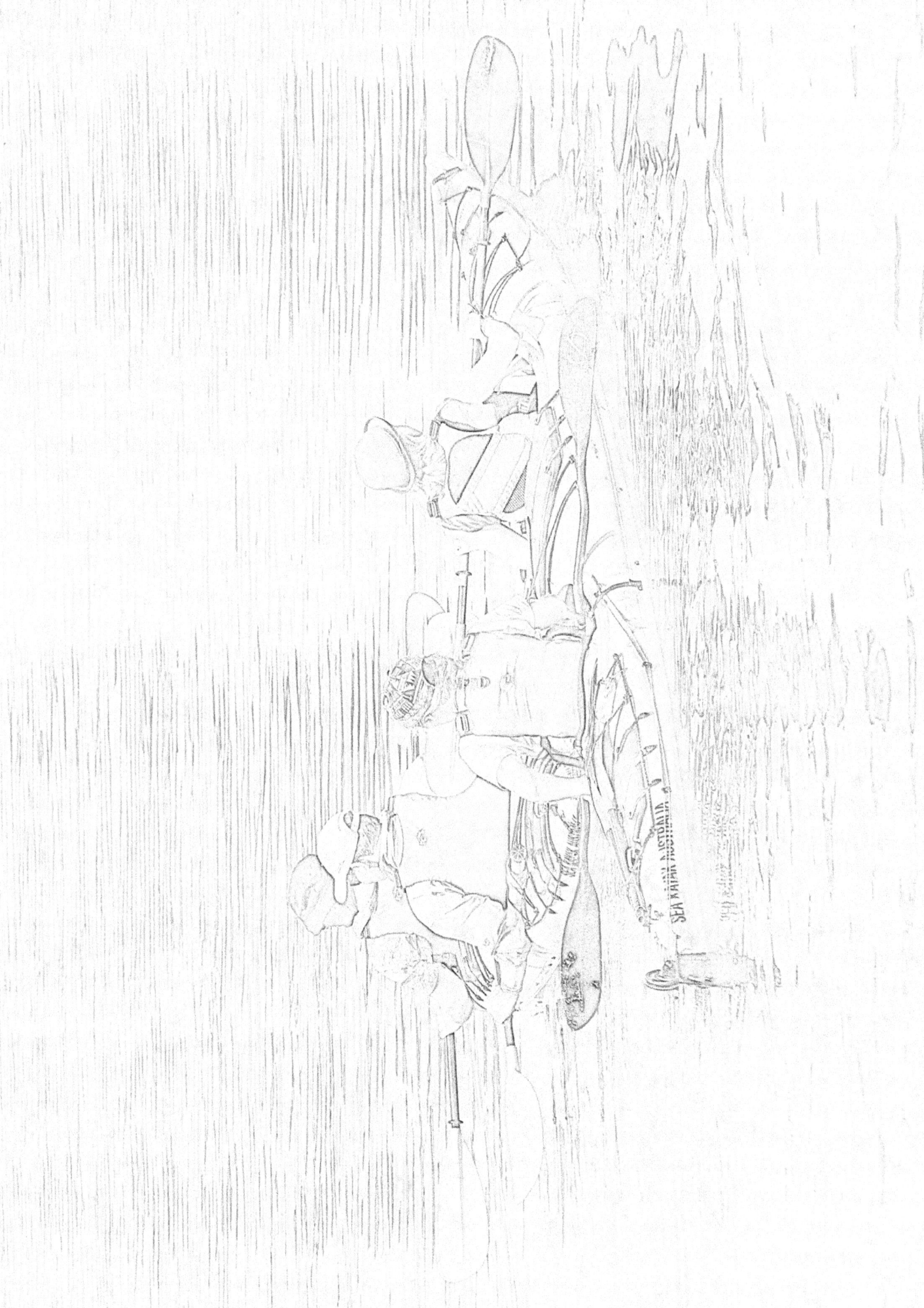

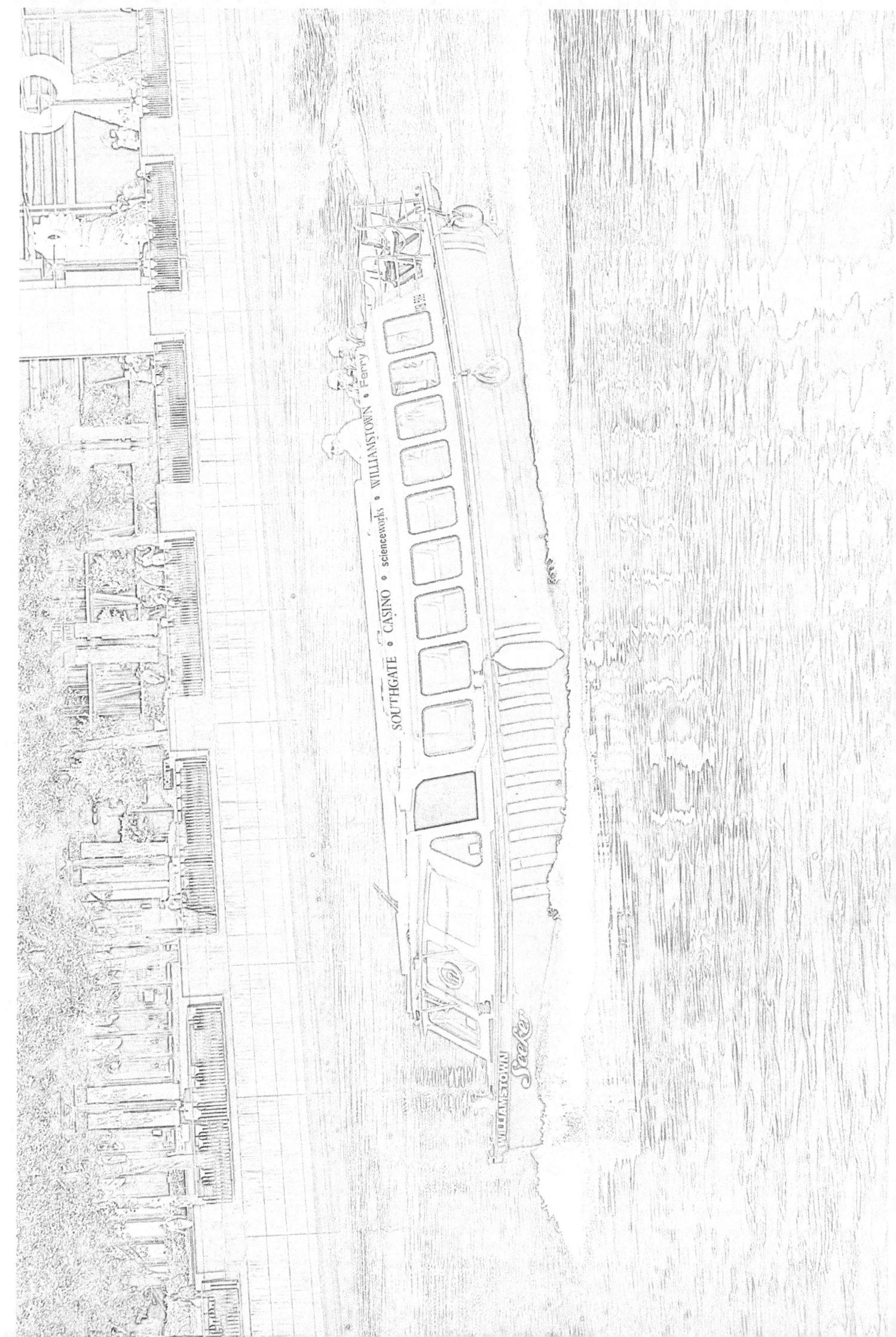

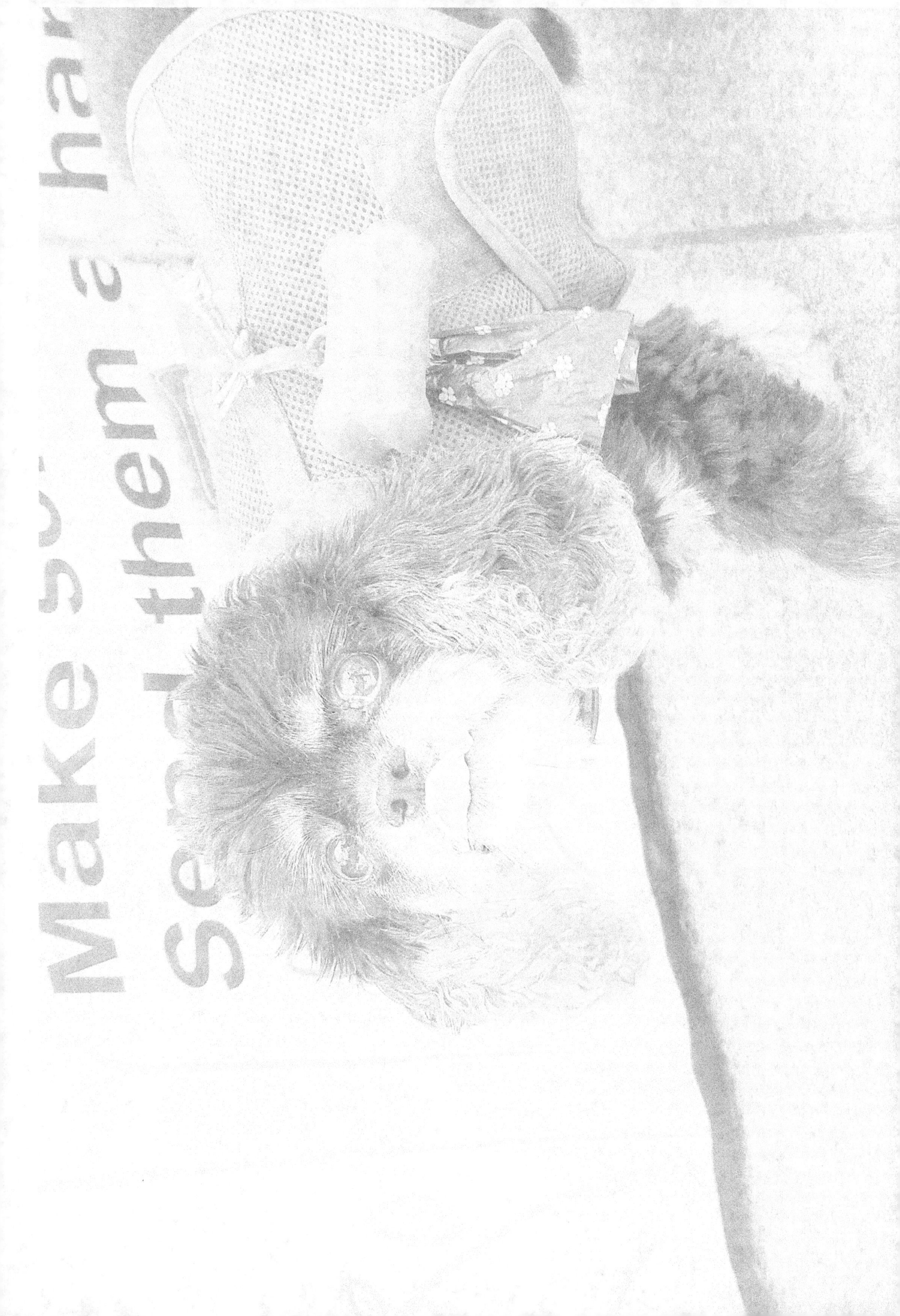

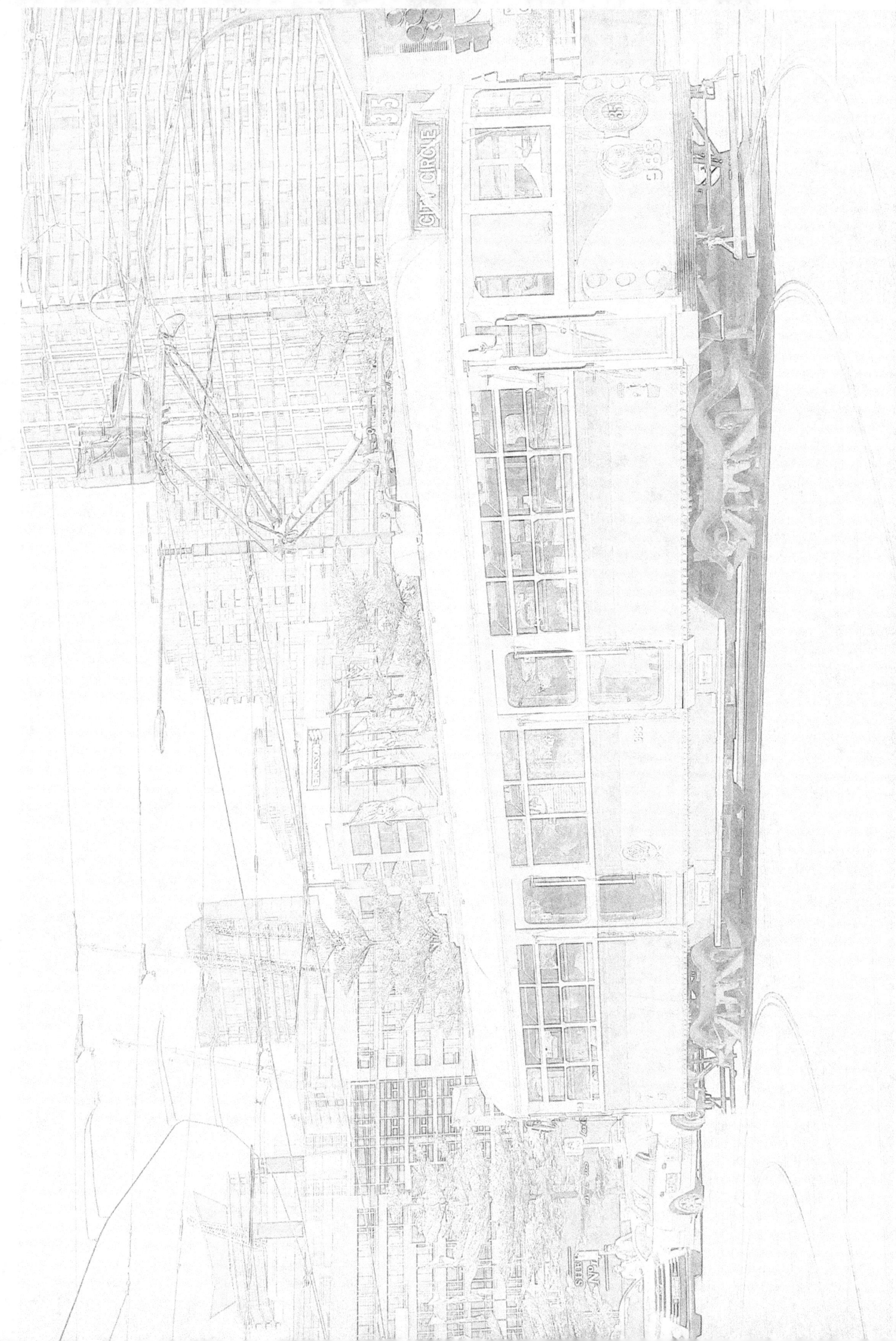

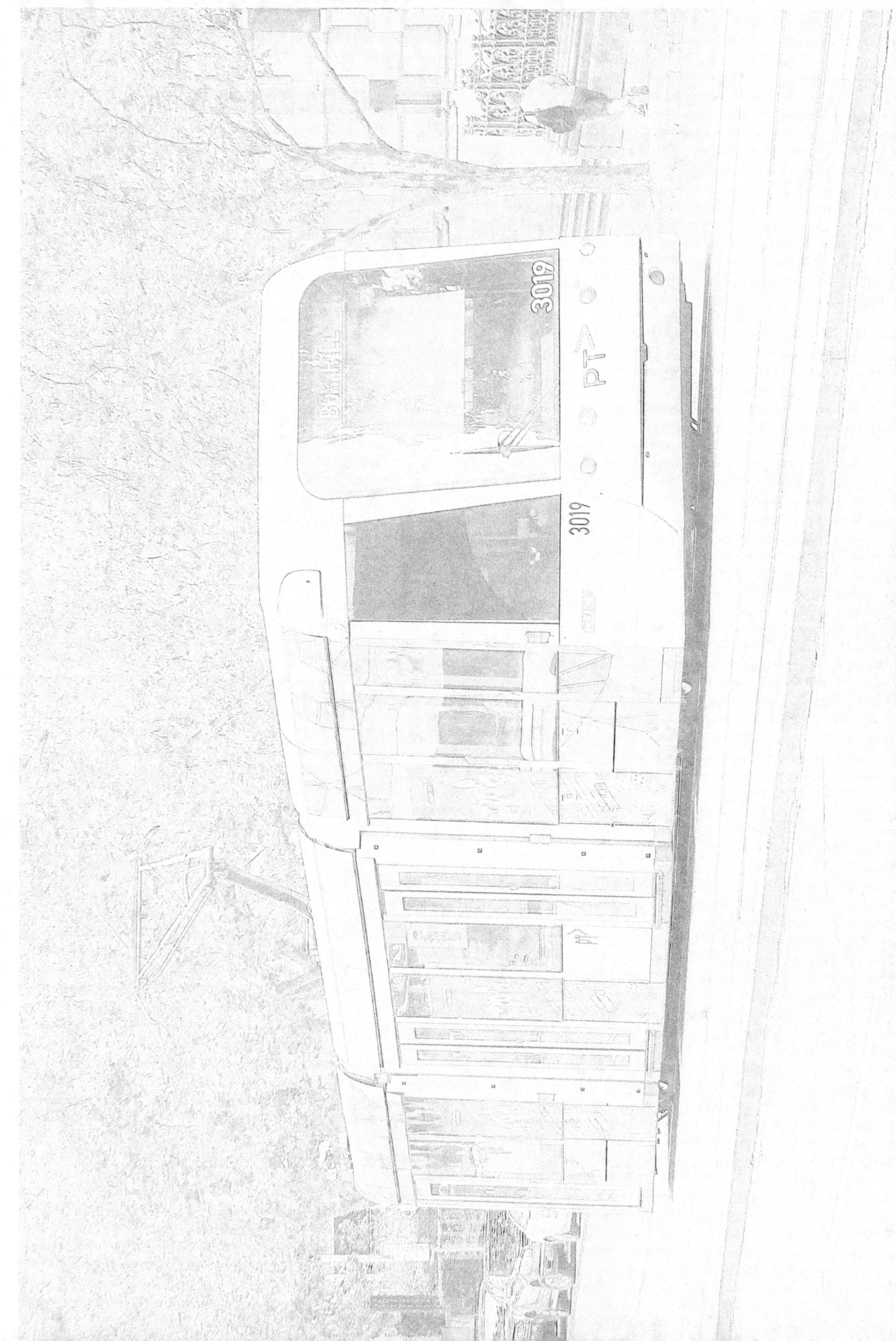

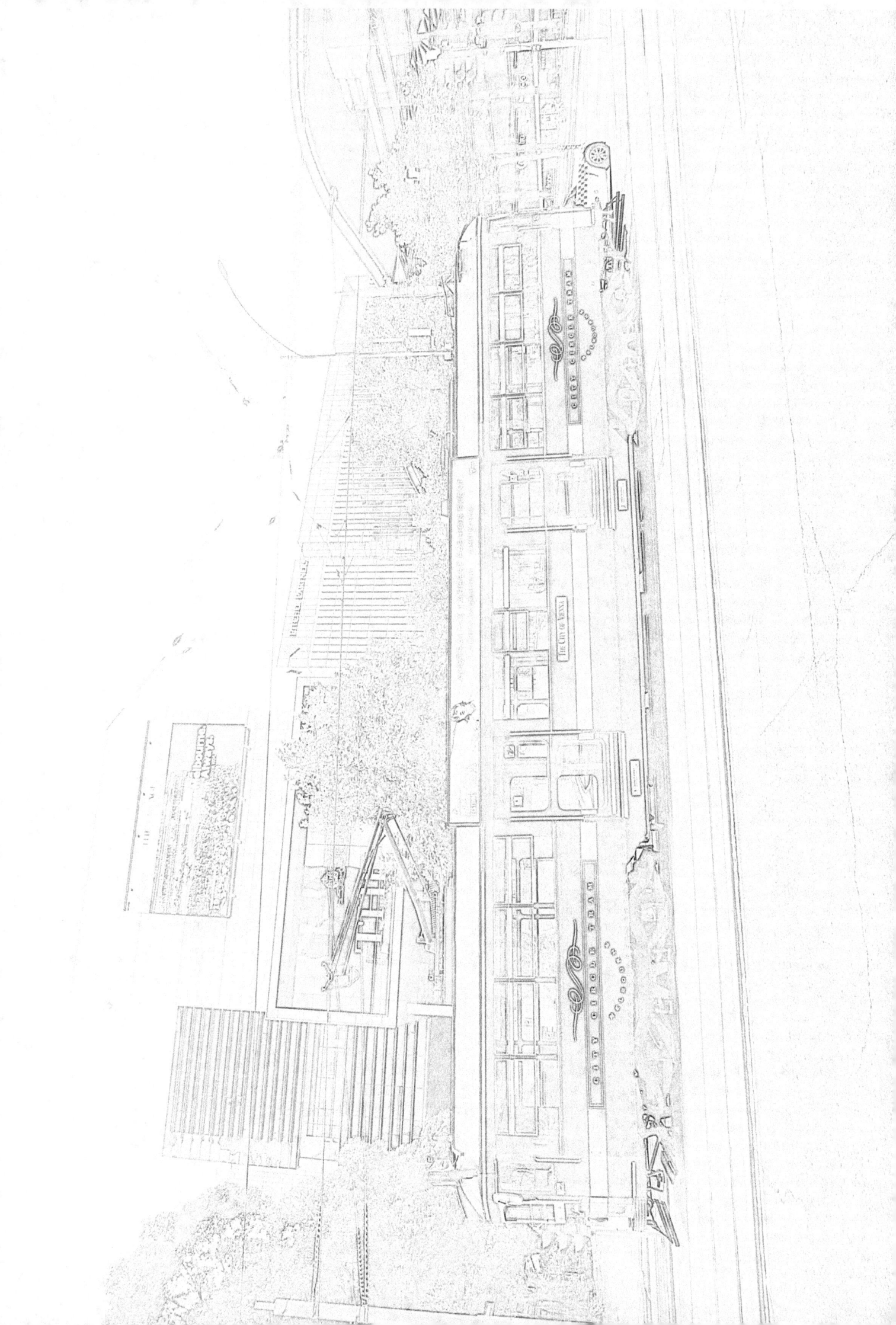

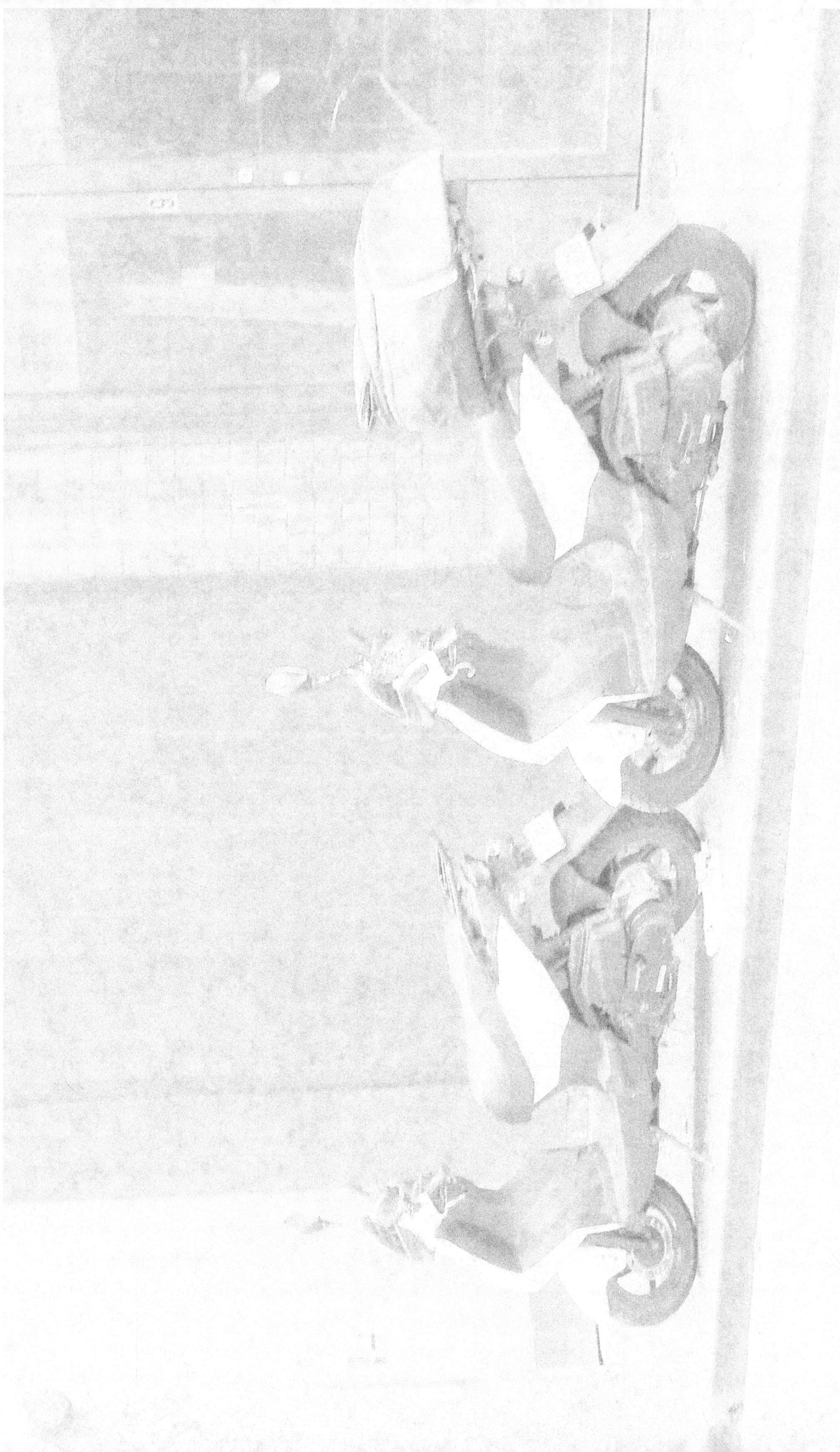

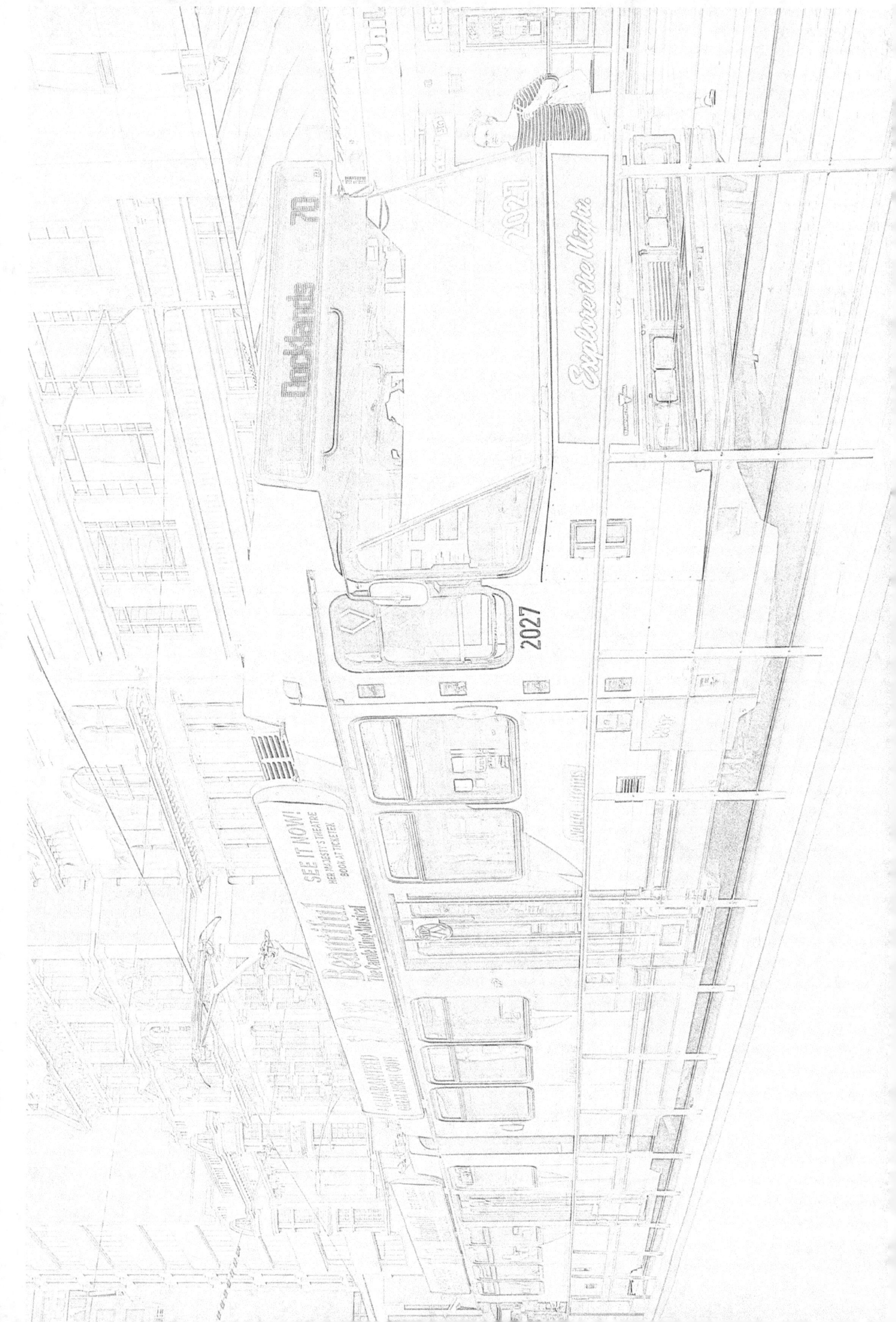

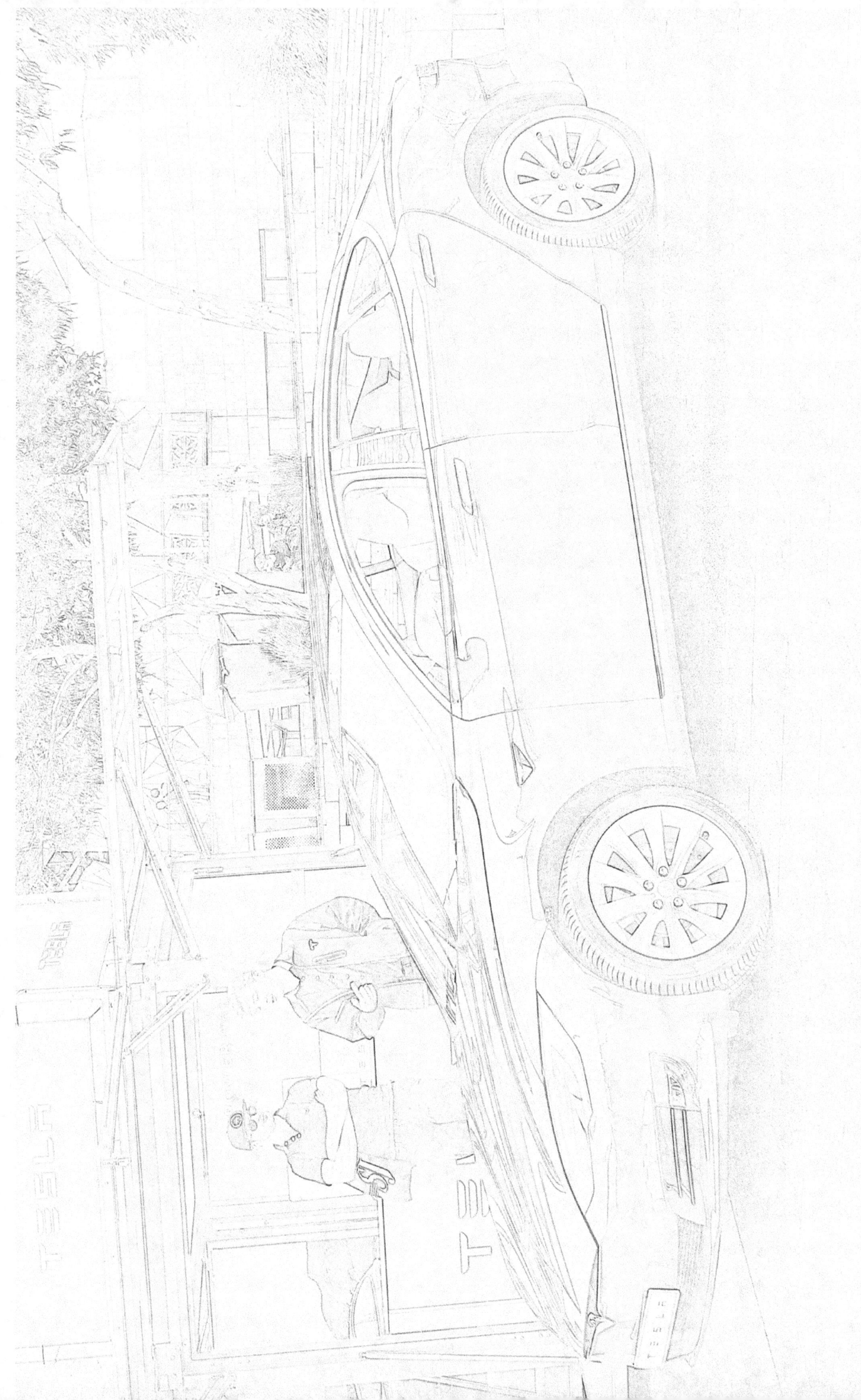

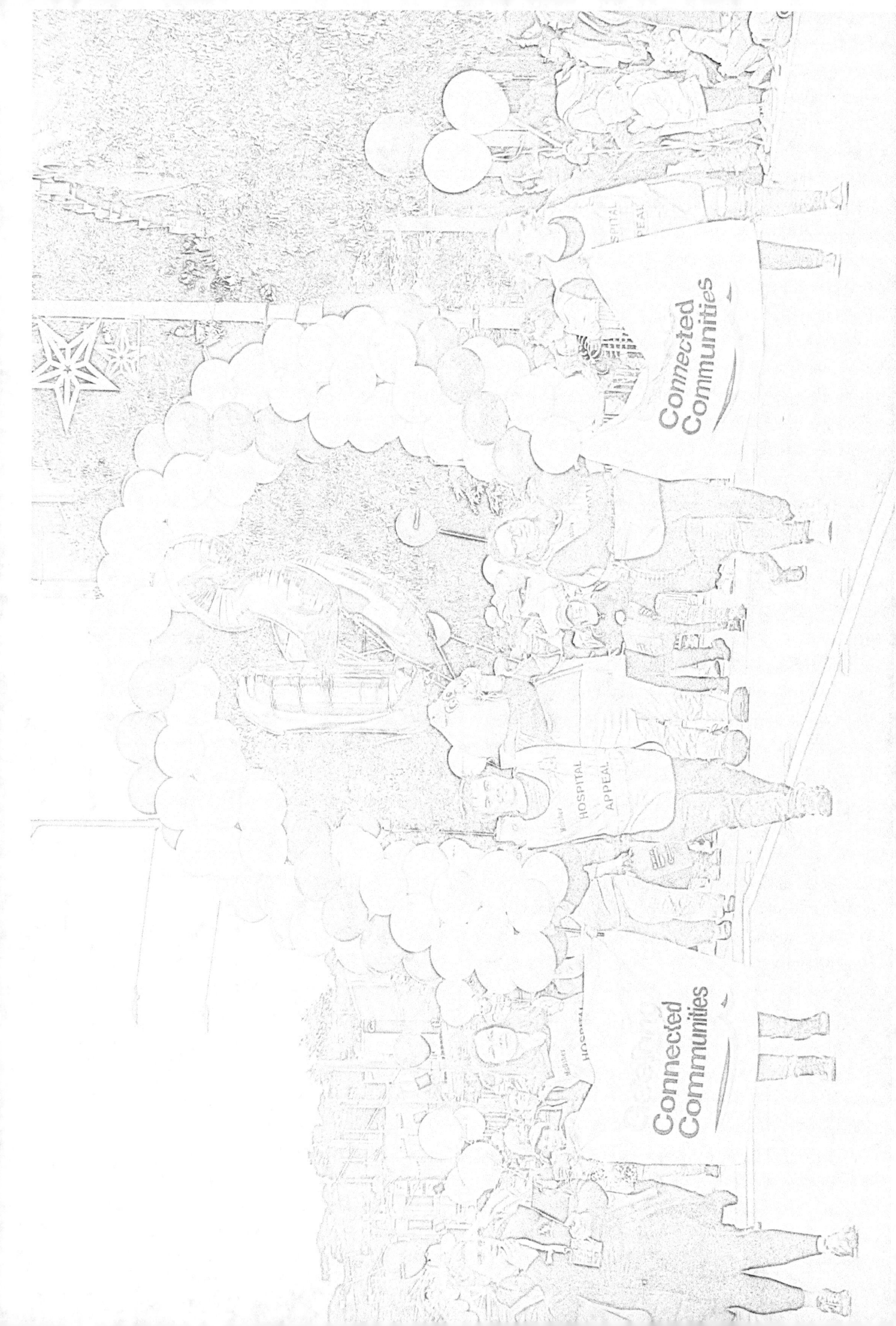

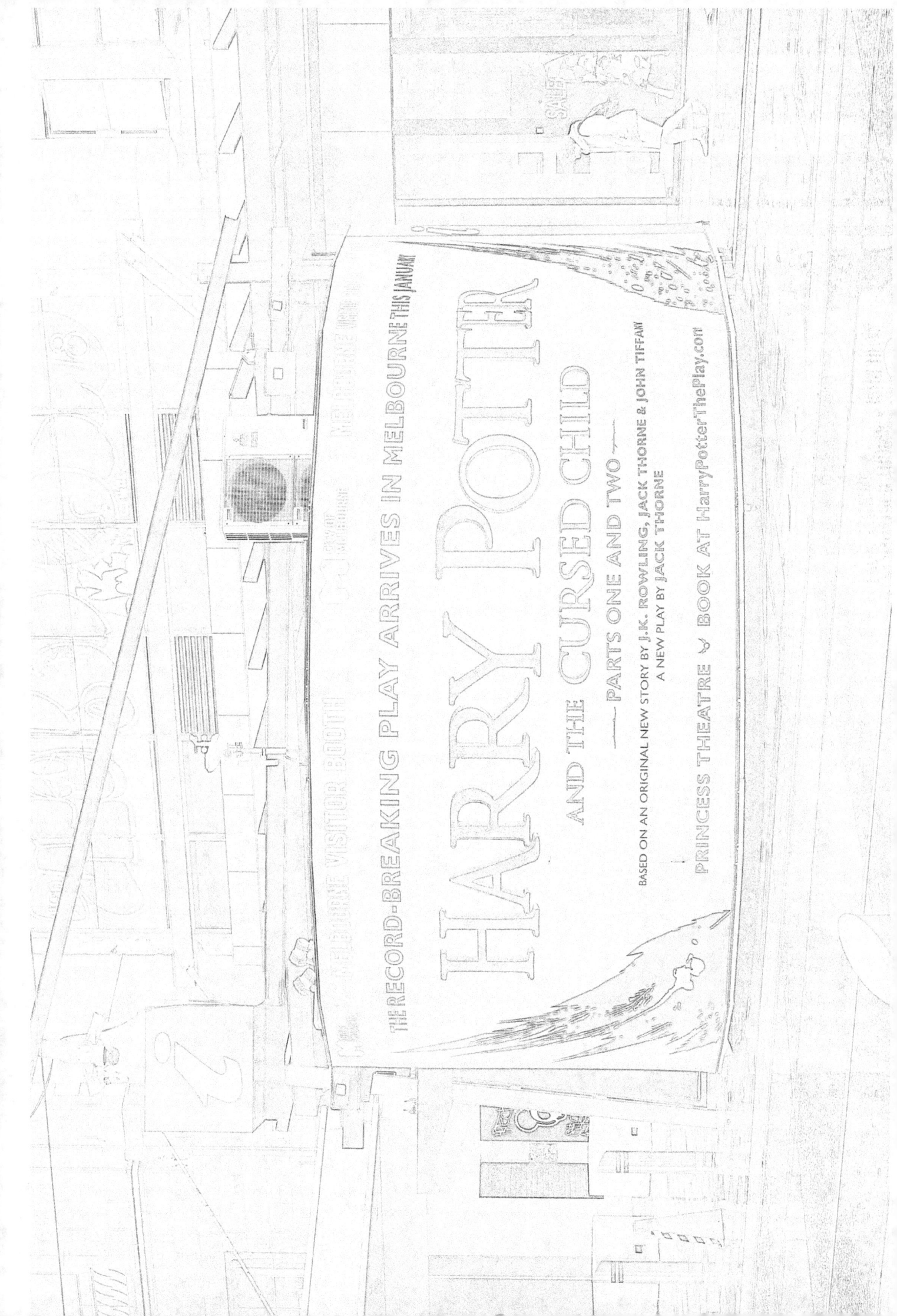

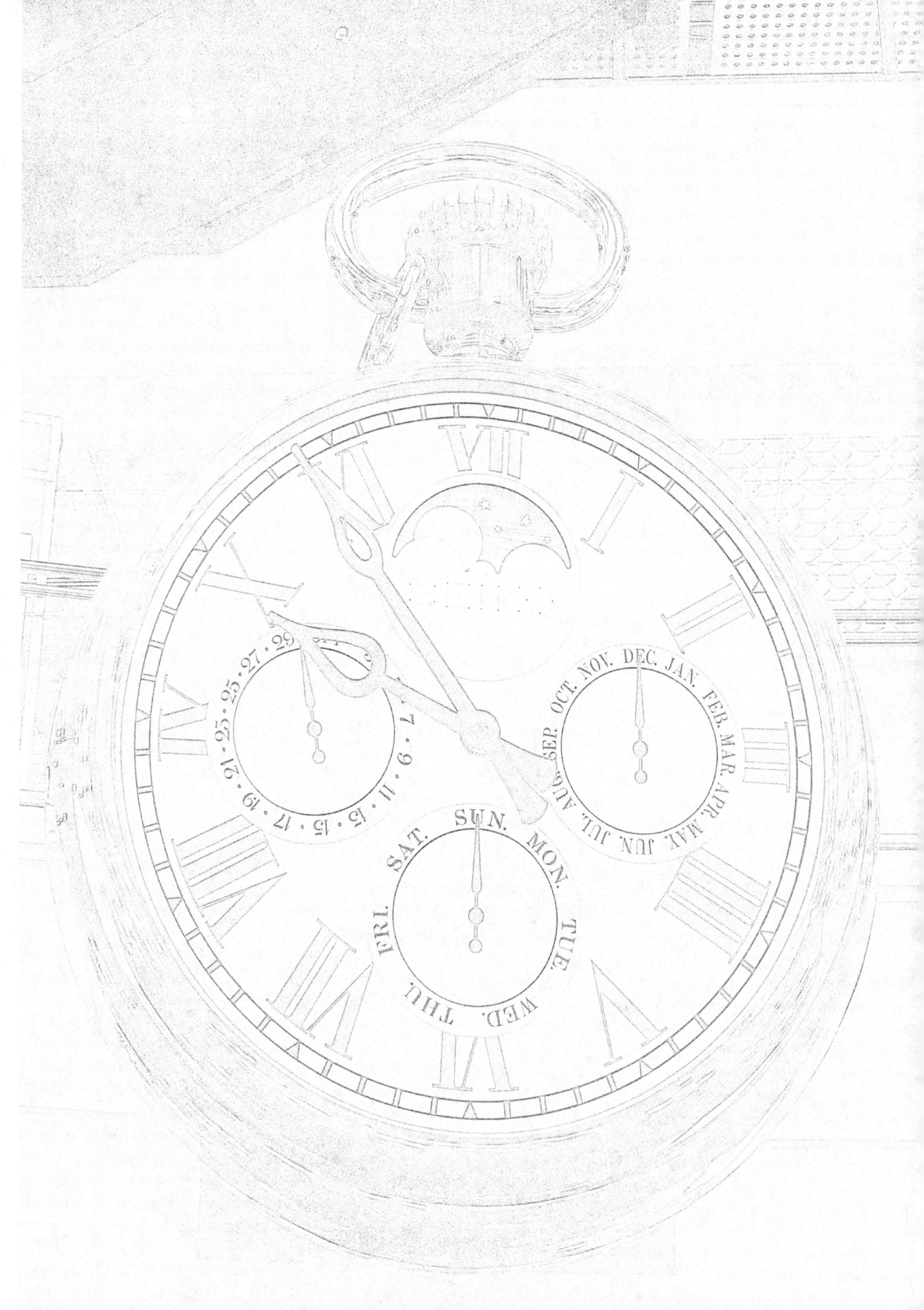

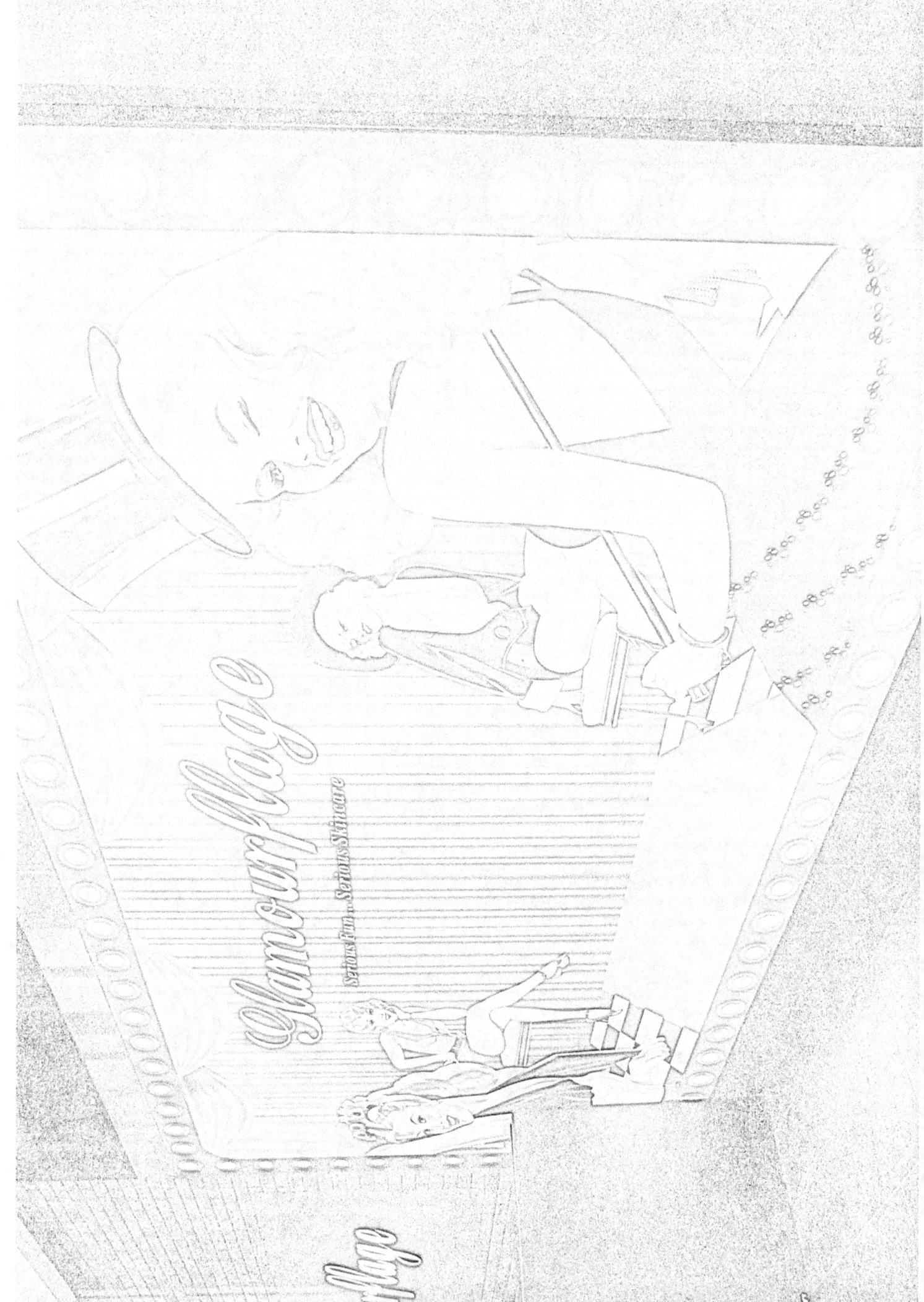

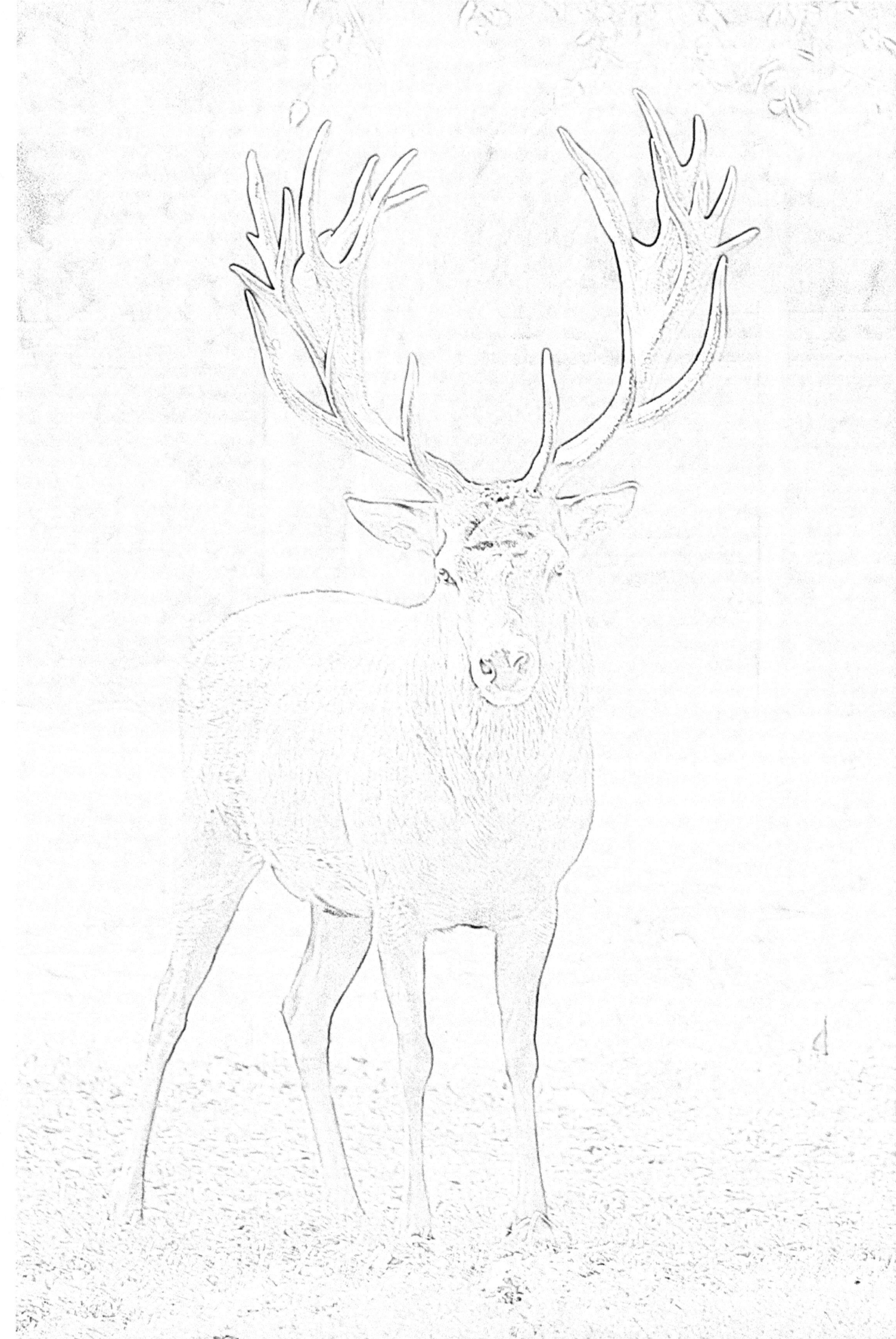

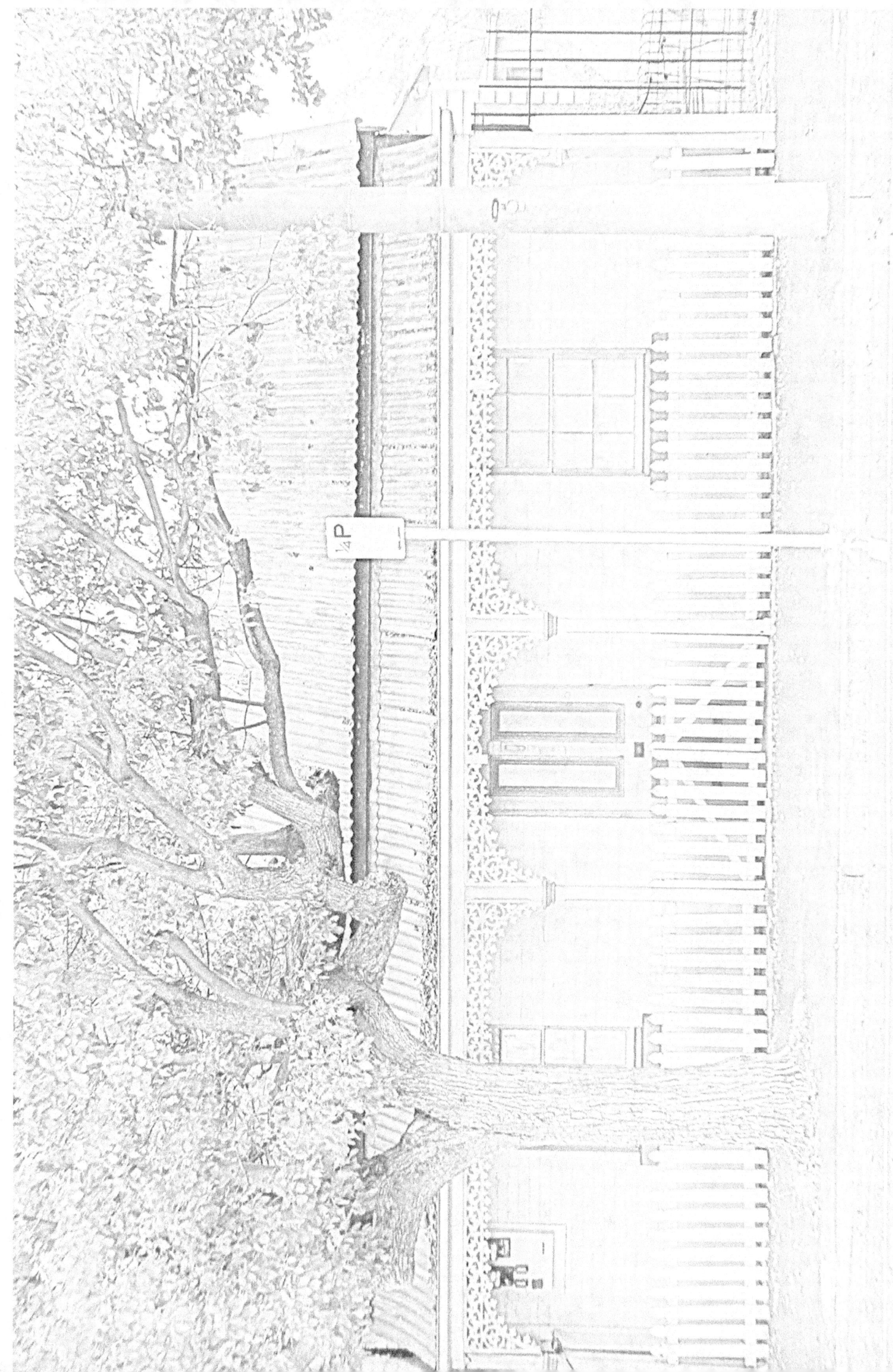

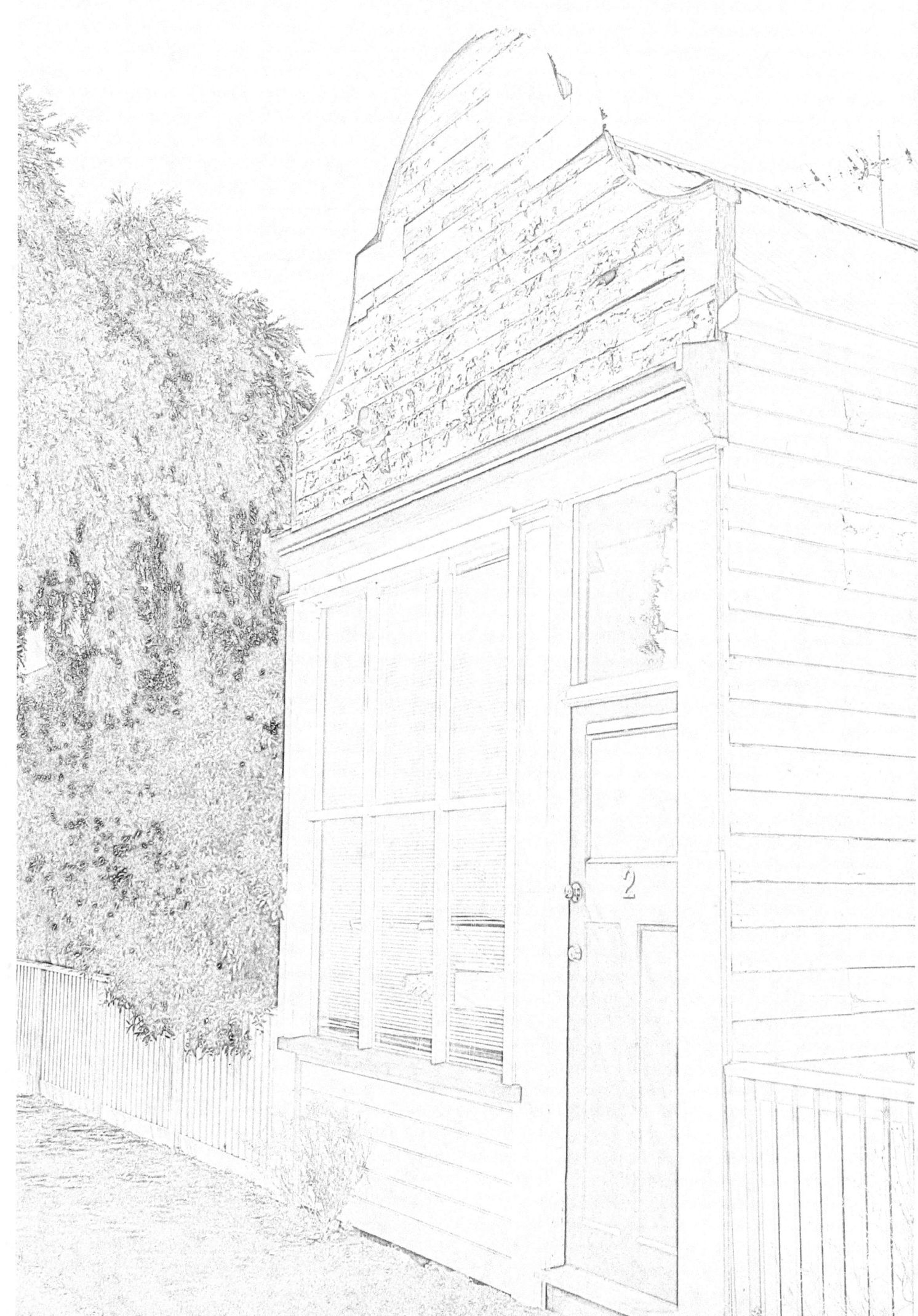

Erected by
NEW ENGLAND RESIDENTS
TO MARK WHERE LIES
THUNDERBOLT
[FRED WARD]